The Producers: Contemporary Curators in Conversation

A series of public events sponsored jointly by the Department of Fine Art, University of Newcastle and the BALTIC Centre for Contemporary Art. The series is organised by Professor Susan Hiller, BALTIC Chair of Contemporary Art and Vicki Lewis, BALTIC Curator and is held in the Fine Art Lecture Theatre at the University. Members of the University and the public are warmly invited to attend.

30th March 2000
James Lingwood and **Sune Nordgren** in conversation
Chaired by Professor John Milner

8th June 2000
Clive Phillpot and **Matthew Higgs** in conversation
Chaired by Sune Nordgren

Edited by Susan Hiller and Sarah Martin

BALTIC   UNIVERSITY OF NEWCASTLE

First published in 2000 by BALTIC in collaboration with the University of Newcastle, Department of Fine Art.

BALTIC
P.O. Box 158, Gateshead, NE8 1FG
Great Britain
www.balticmill.com
ISBN 1-903655-01-3

University of Newcastle
Newcastle upon Tyne, NE1 7RU
ISBN 0-7017-0099-8

Design by Ripe Design Consultancy, The New Inn, Bridge Street, Blaydon-on-Tyne.
Printed and bound in Great Britain by Cox and Wyman Ltd.
Cardiff Road, Reading, Berkshire

ACKNOWLEDGEMENTS

The publishing team and the organisers of this series would like to thank everyone who helped to make the events run smoothly, in particular Brigitte Jurack, Lecturer in Sculpture, University of Newcastle and Dave Pipkin, sound engineer. Thanks also to Sarah Martin for producing the transcripts.

This publication documents two public discussions that took place recently under the combined auspices of the Department of Fine Art at the University of Newcastle and the BALTIC Centre for Contemporary Art in Gateshead. The idea of working together on a series of events emerged from several informal meetings with Andrew Burton (Chair of the Department of Fine Art) and Vicki Lewis (BALTIC Curator) at which we talked about collaborating on projects that would share the facilities and resources of both institutions to expand the context for contemporary art in the North East. The enthusiastic audience response to our idea, and the lively atmosphere of the resulting presentations by distinguished curators contributed to a memorable series of events, which has created a strong foundation for future collaborative projects.

SUSAN HILLER

The Producers: Contemporary Curators in Conversation

CONTENTS

THE PRODUCERS: CONTEMPORARY CURATORS IN CONVERSATION

30TH MARCH, 2000, UNIVERSITY OF NEWCASTLE, DEPARTMENT OF FINE ART.

JAMES LINGWOOD AND SUNE NORDGREN IN CONVERSATION CHAIRED BY PROFESSOR JOHN MILNER

SUSAN HILLER:

Hello and welcome. Just to introduce myself briefly, my name is Susan Hiller and I've recently been appointed to the Chair of the BALTIC Professor of Contemporary Art at the University of Newcastle. Today is the first in a unique series of discussions sponsored jointly by the Department of Fine Art here at the University and the BALTIC Centre for Contemporary Art. The theme of these discussions will be the many and varied approaches to the role of the curator in initiating, commissioning and presenting contemporary art. Some of you will know that it's been said quite a lot in recent years that the curator has replaced the art critic and also the artist, as the central figure in today's world of art. This and other issues will undoubtedly be discussed today and in forthcoming discussions in the series.

So, without further ado I would like to introduce the participants in today's discussion. James Lingwood has been the Co-Director of the London-based arts organisation Artangel since 1991. Artangel commissions have included works as diverse as Rachel Whiteread's 'House', Richard Billingham's 'Fishtank' and Matthew Barney's 'Cremaster'. As an independent freelance curator, James Lingwood has organised many major exhibitions of contemporary art, including a retrospective survey of the works of Robert Smithson, as well as exhibitions by Bernd and Hiller Becher, Thomas Schütte, Juan Munuõz and Thomas Struth.

Sune Nordgren, on the other side of the table, needs no introduction I'm sure. He comes from Sweden and as the first Director of the Baltic Centre for Contemporary Art in Gateshead, he will be playing a leading role in the development of contemporary art in the region as well as internationally. Trained as a graphic designer, he has been a television arts producer, art critic and Director of Malmö Konsthall. There he organised numerous exhibitions of modern and contemporary art, including Francis Bacon, Max Ernst, Cindy Sherman, George Baseltitz and Marlene Dumas, among others. He also initiated and directed the international artists' studio programme (Iaspis) in Stockholm.

Last but not least, Professor John Milner. John is a distinguished Art Historian who has written extensively on Russian art of the early Soviet period, for example Malevich. And more recently, on the art of the Paris Commune. More recently, he has also been involved with curating and organising exhibitions, particularly of art of the early Soviet period. John is the Chair of today's discussion and I turn this over to you.

PROF. JOHN MILNER:

Thank you Susan. I think if you look around this room, already you can see the point of this exercise: there are young artists, there are more established artists, there are museum directors, at least one architect who designs museums, critics and so on, who all have diverse vested interests. So my role in a way is to keep the conversation moving, to intervene sometimes, and to provide, not only an opportunity for the distinguished visitors to give you an idea of what they do and what they stand for, but to raise questions in various broad areas that arise out of the rather startling contrasts in the way that they operate. Sune, with an enormous building and a determination not to collect (Sune: I haven't made up my mind yet. Audience laughter) and James, who eschews the idea really, of a building as something – well, we shall see – that separates out art from life. So there are quite different viewpoints here. I will try to enable questions from the floor, certainly towards the end of this exercise. First of all, James Lingwood is going to introduce us to some of the activities of Artangel and Sune Nordgren will follow on from that. Then we will begin the debate.

JAMES LINGWOOD:

I do want to reiterate that when Susan asked me to participate in this, it was on the basis that this would be a discussion, rather than a lecture; so I'm looking forward to talking together rather than us talking 'at' you. I'd also like to pick up on something John Milner said in his introduction. I don't think that the curator is displacing the artist in the centre of contemporary visual culture. What is happening, I think, is that a present generation of curators sees their relationship as being with artists and not only with works of art or artefacts. The consensus for most of the century has been that curators looked after, they cared for, they conserved, they displayed. The works of art had been created in a world somehow separated from the world they inhabited. In a way, this was based on a mutual suspicion between the artist and the institution. And I don't think that separation attends in the way that contemporary art is organised and produced today, and the degree of suspicion has diminished – not that it will, or indeed should, be totally dispelled. The BALTIC sees itself as a producing organisation, for example, so does the new Tate. The transformation from a more passive mode of housing art, to a more active mode of producing (art works and meanings) has quickened in the past few years within an international cultural economy, which is increasingly competitive. I think what has happened in the past few years is not that the curator has displaced the artist, but that there has been a reorganising of the relations between curator, artist, art critic and art institution and the most significant shift has been the downgrading of the voice (and the power) of independent criticism.

Basically I see Artangel as a kind of medium between the ideas of artists and their realisation in the world. We are fundamentally commissioners and producers, not curators. We have nothing to 'curate', nothing to look after, except for the relationship with an individual artist or a group of artists and their ideas, and the discussion as to where and how those ideas might materialise in the real world.

This means that we do not start with anything on the table. Essentially we begin with a conversation and a respect. As the global art economy grows exponentially, just like the global economy, it does not become more varied, it becomes more consensual. So whilst there is substantial growth in opportunities for artists, this means more opportunities of a similar kind.

There are a lot of unstated conventions at work. I think even the process of commissioning contemporary art over the past two or three decades has also been very consensual. That happens a lot when commissioners of contemporary art – whether they're art agencies or people involved in local government, corporations, arts festivals, biennials or whatever – somehow when the invitation to get involved in a commission is made, what that commission might be is already implicitly limited. There's a kind of ring-fencing or a circumscribing of possibilities. The limits are already inscribed in the initial conversation. Now these limits might be to do with concerns as pragmatic as a kind of material or money or they might be to do with time-scale, physical scale or the situation or location. That's not to say that there aren't limits because you always come up against limits at some point in the artistic process. But it's our aspiration that, with an Artangel commission, we will have pushed the ideas that an artist has and their potentials for meaning to the maximum. There should be no circumscribing of possibility, no short change or quick fix. We will only come up against the limits at the end of the process rather than inscribe them at the beginning. So essentially, in this world of opportunities, we're trying to offer a different kind of opportunity, a different kind of relationship.

(Slide of Rachel Whiteread's 'House', with two pieces of graffiti – 'Wot for?' and 'Why Not!')

I put this slide in to illustrate what I've said about contemporary art and consensus. I don't think contemporary art should be in search of any kind of immediate consensus, as is the case with much art that's been commissioned over the past twenty years. We have to accept that without necessarily seeking to be controversial, we should not avoid its (art's) capacity to be controversial, and not avoid the fact that it will be, in many situations, contentious. And that it will have the potential to generate a vast range of meanings rather than one particu-

lar meaning. And that lack of consensus is an interesting
territory to try to explore.

As I'm going to show you a few slides, it's a good
moment to say that this question of limits is also a
question of frames. Some of these slides are ambiguous,
some might even be duplicitous. Their form replicates one
of the most persistent traditions of Western representa-
tion, which is based on the radical excision of the work
from the world – the frame of the painting marks the end
of the work, and concentrates the viewer's attention within
the boundaries of the frame. That's a very powerful
device, which works to intensify the viewer's experience.
I'm interested in that intensity of experience, but making it
happen in other situations. A large proportion of Artangel's
commissioning takes place in relation to, and indeed is a
part of, a material world. It's not trying to separate itself
from that world. There's no absolute clarity about where
the work might begin and the world might end and vice
versa. There is in a sense, a kind of incorporation of the
world into the work.

I think Rachel Whiteread's 'House' is a good example
of this. A 'frame' is also not only a field of vision, though
that's obviously central, it's a frame of time as well. A
place embodies a number of histories, which may form
part of the material of a work. So I'm talking about what
might be called a relational aesthetic rather than an
autonomous aesthetic. What the next two or three slides
show is that, depending on your particular physical
viewpoint in relation to the sculpture, the reading of the
sculpture would change. From this viewpoint the sculpture
('House'), which is made from one of the terraced houses,
is seen in the context of three different churches, which
encourages a reading about how bourgeois life in the
Victorian era moved from an idea of religion as an organising agent of stability to the idea of domesticity and family
and home. You could then look at different ways in which
local and national government have tried to re-organise

community life from the terraces that had once been in this road, to at the other extreme, the utopian aspirations of the 1960s high rise block which towers over the sculpture from afar. Or again, from North to South, the relationship between the local through to its antithesis in the global: Canary Wharf as a symbol of late-Thatcherite multinational economic re-organising.

All of our projects, or almost all of them, happen in time. The material with which they work pre-exists the actual physical realisation, and then, on the other hand, if they're successful they continue to reverberate for a period of time after the physical work has been removed. So, this is the location where 'House' was. The sculpture itself was only visible for about eighty days or so and then it was knocked down and the area turfed over. But I think for an awful lot of people who visited the sculpture and experienced it, it continues to have a presence in this neutralised landscape. (In response to question from John Milner) I don't think it's a real site of pilgrimage, no. People don't really go to see where the sculpture stood, but if they saw it they may well not see the site in the same way now.

(Slide) This is another work which inhabits or uses the mode of the historical monument: one of the primary references for Whiteread was probably Lutyen's Cenotaph. We've been interested in ways artists can re-invigorate what is a fairly devalued form of contemporary art making. For example, we were very involved in persuading the Royal Society of Arts to set up a scheme for the empty plinth in Trafalgar Square which has now resulted in Mark Wallinger's 'Ecce Homo' being placed there for nine months. A few years ago, we commissioned the German sculptor Stephan Balkenhol to make two sculptures above and in the River Thames. And again I think the slides suggest this idea of a relational aesthetic in distinction to an autonomous work of art. You're reading the sculpture in relation to the various monuments of the city – the cathedrals of religion and power and money – and the flux of the river which the sculpture relates to and incorporates.

The second Balkenhol work was called 'Man on a Buoy', and like Rachel Whiteread's 'House' it only remained in situ for a few weeks. It was quite interesting because unlike the traditional monument, which if it communicates anything is about an idea of enduring values and stability, this sculpture was intrinsically unstable, it moved with the tide and rocked around a lot. There were so many people calling the police complaining that there was a figure stranded in the River Thames, that they were getting very edgy. Then one afternoon a 'have a go hero' on a London cruise dived into the Thames to save it, at which point we had to agree that the sculpture was up for relocation. (Audience laughter) It was a kind of Pyrrhic vistory for naturalism...

The idea of transformation of a site also relates to interiors. We've been interested in the way in which a contemporary artist can inhabit, temporarily, a historical site and either gently, or quite aggressively transform its meanings. (Slide) This was a building called 50 St. James – right in the heart of London's clubland – where the Mexican artist Gabriel Orozco installed, on a sequence of floors, a number of works relating to games and rules and power. (For example) in the Grand Hall on the first floor, he created an oval billiard table. It was a game which the visitors could actually come and play but in which you had to re-invent the rules of the game. Orozco suspended the red ball in the middle of the table, as a kind of symbol of the ball being in the centre of the game, in the centre of the club, in the centre of the city which would have thought itself to be at the centre of the world at that time. And as you played, you struck the red ball, which would rotate off the edges of this kind of idealised view of the world and gently operate as a pendulum. That idea came from the famous experiment 'Foucault's pendulum', which demonstrated visibly that the world was constantly spinning on an axis and was in motion. In a quiet and elliptical way Orozco awoke the sleeping building and questioned the values which were implicit in that building. The visitor moved through several floors of the building, looking at Orozco's interventions, sometimes playing, sometimes watching people play. Again, the artist incorporated the building as much as the building housed the work.

Not dissimilarly, another 19th-century building is the Roundhouse in Camden Town, which had been built by Stephenson for the purpose of turning round, on an enormous turntable, engines which had come from the North of England, so that they could go back to the North. So the building is a sort of vast industrial cathedral, an emblem of Victorian ideas and beliefs of 'progress'. It was a perfect situation for a visionary project by the Soviet artist Ilya Kabakov, working with his wife Emilia, called 'The Palace of Projects'. This was a kind of tragi-comic version of an idea of a Great Exhibition, or World Fair, of a Project of a Central Cultural Committee, or indeed a Millennium Dome – a celebration and a critique of utopian thinking. Inside this grand wooden structure were projects by some sixty five fictional Soviet citizens, from chauffeurs and doctors to psychologists, artists, teachers, all of which were proposing ideas about how to make yourself a better person or how to make the world a better place. And the moment you thought the project was getting too comic, you realised it was deadly serious, and vice versa. As you climbed up some ridiculously grand stairs to the second floor, you also saw towards the all seeing glass eye in the centre of the roof of the Roundhouse, and the final frame before you descend again was established in Kabakov's design to offer a view of the Roundhouse's own wooden structure as well as to show that the building project, like the project of building a new world, always remains unfinished.

This is now going to be very shorthand. We've also worked on trying to push the boundaries of what artists can do with film and video. We've made two feature-length films as well as a forty-minute programme for television, Richard Billingham's 'Fishtank' which was made with Illuminations for BBC2. In the future it looks as if Artangel will have an ongoing relationship with Channel 4. This is not to supply those disappointing two-minute slots that artists sometimes get given as crumbs on the table, but actually to carve out real space for truly original and innovative media works to be made.

Our first film project was with Matthew Barney. (Slide) I'm using this one as an example because it was another way in which a site was incorporated into a work. The primary material for the first of the 'Cremaster' films were the myths and symbols of the Isle of Man, beginning with the three-legged Manx man, through to the TT races, the idea of the Manx Fairy recreated by three women body builders, underground sea-gods that were felt to inhabit the areas around the island, and the Loughtonon Candidate, the indigenous sheep on The Isle of Man. The work was a forty five-minute film. But the way in which Barney inhabits and transforms that form is truly extraordinary.

Another very different film project was with Douglas Gordon. He took as his primary material, not a physical location or site but a film. And the film was Hitchcock's 'Vertigo'. We made a new film, based on a new recording of Bernard Herrmann's score, which is one of the most extraordinary film scores ever written. Gordon's film was based entirely on the features of the conductor of a new version of the score, James Conlon from the Paris Opera, as he was leading – or was he acting, it was never quite clear? – an orchestra. The work was then installed in an enormous space at the top of an industrial building (Atlantis Gallery, Brick Lane, London). You had to ascend to it up a staircase reminding you of the ascent and descent in 'Vertigo' itself. An enormous cinema-scale image was suspended in the middle of this dark cavernous space. And right at the back of the space, a small video projection of 'Vertigo' itself. The new and the old films moved in and out of synch.

And one final work, which at this moment is the only Artangel piece that you can experience, and which is also very concerned with the relationship between sound, memory and an experience of the city. This is a work by the Canadian artist Janet Cardiff called 'The Missing Voice (Case Study B)' which takes you from the crime section of Whitechapel Library, out into the streets of the city in a kind of fragmentary narrative, drawing on a range of genres from film noir to detective stories to city guides. You begin this work by borrowing a discman at the Library, and you end up some forty minutes later in the concourse of Liverpool Street station. The city is hers and it is yours.

The theme I'm trying to thread through this is incorporation...the place and the city become part of the artwork and inseparable from it. I think in a much more low-key way, Janet Cardiff's piece embodies this idea of incorporation no less strongly than Rachel Whiteread's 'House'.

(Audience applause)

SUNE NORDGREN:

I do hope that James is right: that there is a shift in the relationship between artists and curators, because I think that it (the promotion of the curator) has gone too far, and you still see every week invitation cards where the curator's name is mentioned but not the artist's. So, let's hope there is a shift. Certainly, for me and my vision for the BALTIC and the way the BALTIC team will be working, we will always put the artist at the centre. It will be a place where exhibitions will be shown – international collaborations and so on – but I also foresee that several of the exhibitions and artworks you will see at the BALTIC will be generated here: at the BALTIC and around the BALTIC and there will always be four-five artists working in the building.

(Slides) The first artist I commissioned – my first serious international commission I should say – was with the English artist Richard Long, in Malmö Konsthall. I was not yet the Director at that time, but a sort of Guest Curator and was invited to do a one-person show for their main space – a beautiful and simple space. A few years before I had seen Richard's exhibition at the Venice Biennial – this was in 1976 when he represented Britain – and I invited him to Malmö to do a piece. He created a fantastic site-specific work and as always, at that time at least, he took material from the place where he was working. Outside Malmö there was a chalk quarry, and as you know geologically, chalk is found in layers with flint, so when they take up the chalk they throw away the flint and you are left with mountains of this black and white stone. When Richard was selecting the stones and pulling every-thing together he was attacked by magpies, so he named this line, which is 11m long and 3.5m wide, 'The Magpie Line' and it's now in a collection in Germany. But he also made some enormous mud circles. For those, he brought the mud from the River Avon in Bristol where he lives (Slide). It was basically the artist himself, in a high cherry picker with a good driver down at the floor, and he (Long) just shouted 'left…right…up…down' and then worked with his bare hands directly on the walls to make these beautiful rings. After six weeks we washed the whole thing down, as always with these temporary pieces by Richard Long. But it was well documented and a wonderful memory for me and all the people who saw it. It was also a very good start for me as an 'International Curator'.

(Slide) In 1990 I became the Director of Malmö Konsthall and one of the first artists I invited was Toshikatsu Endo, an exciting Japanese artist. I commis-sioned him to do three works: one inside the gallery and two in a park very close to the Konsthall. He works very much with wood, earth, water and fire; with long wooden logs that he burns and he also puts water into them. Malmö Konsthall is, as I said, a very simple place: rough wooden floors, white walls and beautiful light. That's it. A perfect space for Toshikatsu Endo's nature-based work and he really created a symbiosis between the art and the architecture. The design of the building is based on the ideas and the shape of the ideal artist's studio. The architect Klas Anshelm had one particular studio in his mind, Brancusi's studio in Paris. This was reconstructed and installed in 1977 outside Centre Pompidou in Paris, but it was soon closed and has now been re-installed and designed by Renzo Piano. It's really beautiful now – and it works. It's exactly the same shape, the same proportions and the same idea as at Malmö Konsthall. Of course, these are experiences that I've brought to BALTIC, with its simplicity and its flexibility. We will have the studio-like honesty, the beautiful light and we will of course also have a Swedish wooden floor.

(Slide) In 1994, it was a lousy summer in Sweden – just rain, rain, rain – except for two weeks in late May. For those two weeks we worked outdoors in a camp with Antony Gormley to produce his first really big 'Field', which was a beautiful and fantastic experience, a socially inclusive work which involved a lot of people. We produced 40,000 small clay figures, and everyone was keen to take part: people came from schools and factories around this little village where the brick factory and our camp were placed, just outside Malmö. The clay in the southern part of Sweden is very hard, so the figurines were not really like human beings, they were more ghost-like. The reduction of the oxygen during fixing made some of the figures pretty dark, so all together they became almost like a blood stream running down the space. This first big Field was called the 'European Field'. For this exhibition I collaborated with Tate Liverpool and IMMA

(Irish Museum of Modern Art) in Dublin. But Liverpool produced their own Field, called 'Field for the British Isles', also 40,000 figures, which was shown here in Gateshead a few years later. The field that we produced – the 'European Field' – went on a tour in Europe on its own. It toured Central and Eastern Europe and the Baltic countries for over a year and came back to Malmö Konsthall where it is now part of their collection.

Before the exhibition with Antony Gormley in 1994, I went to his studio in London and saw these enormous pieces (slide) hanging from the ceiling and standing on the floor. They were in plaster and not very heavy – a couple of hundred pounds perhaps. But he couldn't get them out of the studio because they were too big: he had to take down a wall to get them out. Antony said, 'it doesn't matter anyhow because it's a piece that will never be realised, it's impossible. I want to do them in cast iron and no one in the world is stupid enough to want to commission this'. But there was a Swedish person who was stupid enough to do it. (Audience laughter) And I don't regret it! These so called 'Expansion Pieces' were cast in a foundry in Halifax and one of the sculptures, 'Body', in the new cast-iron version, weighs five and a half tonnes and another one, 'Earth' weighs eight tonnes. There were actually five pieces in total. This hanging piece of course couldn't hang from the ceiling: there was a crane behind the Konsthall, which went down through the ceiling, so it could hang like this. The piece, 'Fruit', (slide) is now in Japan and was only one and a half tonnes. So this was my second commission with Antony Gormley and it was shown in the same exhibition together with the first Field.

(Slide) In 1994 I managed to get some money to renovate the Konsthall, so it had to be closed for eight weeks. But I didn't want it to be closed for such a long period, so I commissioned Barbara Kruger to do an artwork outside and around Malmö. We managed to get very good sponsorship from a national billboard company, which meant that it was also shown in 1,300 other places all over Sweden, on about 5000-6000 big billboards. The enormous poster just said 'Think Like Us', 'Talk Like Us', 'Love Like Us', 'Hate Like Us', 'Look Like Us' and 'Live Like Us' and at the bottom it said 'an exhibition by Barbara Kruger for Malmö Konsthall'. This was just before the general elections in Sweden, so everyone though it was a political poster. There were guesses about which party it could be who had put them up. In one place in Sweden it was vandalised, and they wrote 'racism' over it: they said there were only white people in the photographs. Unfortunately Barbara had used an image from a baseball game in America, which made it look like a white sport, but we did mange to find some black people in it (the photo), so it wasn't really true. But this shows how differently people interpreted the poster, because the whole situation in Sweden at that time was so politicised.

As I said, Malmö Konsthall is a simple and a very flexible space, so it can be used also for other things. Very often I commissioned artists to do other kinds of artworks, like music, dance etc. together or in connection with the exhibitions. (Slide) So this is a Swedish dance company who did a special performance for the Andres Serrano show in Malmö Konsthall. Focusing on his series of homeless people in New York and the Ku Kux Klan portraits, the dancers performed a partly improvised piece about racism and resistance.

Nancy Spero made a very special piece for us, printing and painting directly on the wall. This was just after the renovation and for that exhibition, the whole Konsthall was divided into two sections: one was very light and open, for Nancy, and the other part was dark, and for that section I commissioned Christian Boltanski to make a new work. He put up two hundred and fifty lockers borrowed from a regiment in Sweden which were arranged to replicate the shape of a street in Malmö. So we invited the nine hundred families from this street to come and look for their house number. They opened the door and their names were on the inside and we asked them to bring some personal items, anything really, to put into the metal lockers. So we got things like wedding dresses, old records, loose teeth, everything…. And it became a kind of collective memory, or 'museum' for this street – Museum Södra Förstadsgatan. The contrast and confronting halves of the Konsthall worked very well. Light against dark, female against male…and the space showed again what new potential it had after the renovation.

(Slide) My last exhibition in Malmö was 'Betong', which is the Swedish word for concrete. Three artists were invited to participate: Miroslaw Balka, Antony Gormley and Anish Kapoor. For this very special exhibition based on one material, Miroslaw Balka created a piece based on his childhood house, where he now has his studio. But he turned the roof the other way so it looked instead like a prison wall. We, on the outside, are locked in and the freedom is inside…

Again, Antony Gormley was involved in this exhibition – my third major commission with him – and he made a piece with three hundred small houses, which all had the shape of a shell for an individual person. We measured three hundred people from the age of one up to eighty six. They fitted into those houses and put together in the Konsthall they looked like Manhattan or Sao Paulo. The work, called 'Allotment', weighs over two hundred tonnes and so has unfortunately not been shown elsewhere.

The third artist in "Betong" was Anish Kapoor and it was the first time I'd worked with him. Another fantastic artist and another fantastic experience which of course grounded a relationship that made it possible for me to go back to him – at short notice – and commission him for the 'Taratantara' work he made for BALTIC last year.

I came to Gateshead in 1996 during the Visual Arts Year, and together with Iwona Blazwick and Declan McGonagle, I was invited to commission an artist. I invited

Jaume Plensa – a Catalan sculptor from Barcelona – to make an artwork. (Slide) He produced a very beautiful lightbeam called 'Blake in Gateshead'. It was lit in November '96, just before the lottery application went in for the BALTIC. And I think this is one of the reasons we got the money, because this lightbeam was visible all the way down to London. (Audience laughter) We kept this light and it will be re-installed for the opening and lit for all major events at BALTIC.

And then last summer, BALTIC commissioned Anish Kapoor to make a new work for the eight-week intermission between the demolition phase and the main contract. He produced a fantastic artwork, where he used the hollowed-out building as part of the piece. It became a fantastic symbiosis of art and architecture. This was not just an impressive and brilliant sculpture, with the house and the PVC structure suspended inside, it was also like bringing life back to the derelict building. And a signal for the future of the level and quality of work that we want to do at BALTIC and of the way we want to work with artists – to create new site-specific work that you have to come to Gateshead to see.

And in the near future, two more artists: For November (2000) we've commissioned Dutch artist Marijke van Warmerdam to make a new 35 mm film that will be shown in a busy public place in the region. This (slide) is a permanent video installation by her at the Schiphol airport in Amsterdam, of a man taking a shower. Before that, in October, we will commission Jenny Holzer to do a series of works – projections on buildings will be the main and most spectacular part of it, but also using other media, like the BALTIC newsletter and interventions in public places. So it will be very present here in the region. Again, something to look forward to. (Audience applause)

PROF. JOHN MILNER (CHAIRING THE DISCUSSION):

In a way, Sune, since the BALTIC project began, you have had a great building project on your hands but one which wasn't ready for exhibiting anything. But in a lot of what you were showing from Malmö – and it was evident from your tone really – you took a great delight in a controlled atmosphere, the material of the Kunsthalle. So do you feel, a little like James, that you have at the moment a gallery without a gallery; that you're operating in a public space? In other words, perhaps one thing we could discuss first is what I think of as the 'outer skin'- where does the gallery end? How welcoming is it or how far does it penetrate the space outside, because you're 'homeless' in a physical sense?

JAMES LINGWOOD:

I think the relationship between control and contingency is interesting. We want the artists we work with to be able to realise their vision in as precise a way as possible, but at the same time the readings of the work, the readings the work will generate, will be contingent upon other consider-ations beyond the artistic control. That might be to do with the physical environment or the political environment. But I think that 'grit' is of interest, or can be of interest.

PROF. JOHN MILNER

But it's quite different from the way I believe Sune described the beam of light sculpture to the politicians. In a sense, there's a regeneration of a whole area, there's local pride, all kinds of things in a building project...

JAMES LINGWOOD:

Sune has responsibilities and political imperatives to deal with for sure, which at Artangel we tend to try and circum-navigate because we only materialise in a particular location for a particular length of time. We don't have those kinds of pressure to contend with. We have other kinds of pressure.

SUNE NORDGREN:

But even after, when the BALTIC is open, I don't see it very much as an 'institution' – it is an institution of course. But since we are here, and not in central London, it's very important for me that BALTIC is very transparent, and this institution, so to speak, is more like a generator... I very much want it to be like an 'arts factory'.

PROF. JOHN MILNER:

So you see a kind of tension with the monumentality of the building? The regeneration of the riverbank going on around it...

SUNE NORDGREN:

It's a very prominent building of course, and it's in one way quite stupid to build an arts centre in a building like that if you're really honest. It's a vertical building, which is always problematic. But it's there, and there is an affection for the building, there are lots of reasons to keep it and it's now a part of a much, much bigger scheme than it was when BALTIC was thought of ten years ago. So of course, it's not only about accepting it, it's also about using it in a very, very active way.

PROF. JOHN MILNER:

It's a great monument in itself, which means all sorts of things...

SUNE NORDGREN:

Which means you also have to work against it in a way...

PROF. JOHN MILNER: (TO JAMES LINGWOOD)

And you live without (a building) quite happily?

JAMES LINGWOOD:

We live without. I do think that probably in the late 60s and 70s there was a sense that radical artistic practices were aimed directly against the institution. And we should accept now that for one reason or another those institutions have been fairly effective in appropriating those practices and indeed most of the artists who created them have also been – and are happy to have been – absorbed into the bodies of the institution. The artists with whom we work today and – (to audience) probably many of you as artists as well – think about their work in these different kinds of situations – inside the white box and outside in the rougher world – without necessarily having this sense of the one being in opposition to the other, which might have existed in previous generations. And artists just move with considerable fluidity or dexterity between these situations. So we can't really construct an oppositional world in the way that we could have done twenty five years ago.

PROF. JOHN MILNER:

Does this idea of monumentality or an outer edge effect your audience? You were both talking about projects that had very wide coverage and a very warm and varied response from a lot of people. (To Sune) You don't want the walls of the BALTIC to enclose people; you want to reach out beyond that...?

SUNE NORDGREN:

Well, it's a meeting place as well for people

PROF. JOHN MILNER:

So is there a special relationship?

JAMES LINGWOOD:

Well, I think what can happen with some of our projects in relation to the idea of audience – and I think this is where they're most effective – is when you have a combination of what you would call an intentional audience, who come to that work with prior knowledge of the artists or of Artangel, or prior knowledge of the vocabularies of contemporary art. So, you have that intentional audience on the one side and on the other side you have the incidental audience, which may encounter the work for any number of reasons without bringing to it the same kind of vocabularies that an informed constituency will. That creates, I think, a particularly interesting chemical mix if you like. I think the BALTIC will generate that kind of combination of intentional and incidental as well, because it will certainly have a tremendous magnetic pull on people who are curious, without necessarily having the same framework to re-work critically, that most people here would have. I guess we are both interested in that sort of mixture of audiences.

SUNE NORDGREN:

Well, I could throw out a fire…to the public of course. Because when I came here, my first night in Newcastle was the closing night of the Zone (Photography) Gallery and I heard immediately that this was because of the BALTIC. This is how I was met here. There is – you shouldn't call it hostility anymore – a little bit of fear about what this monumental institution will do; everything else will just disappear. I hope, during the two years I've been here, building up the team and being visible, that we can create this feeling of being a kind of generator. Because in London you have Tate Modern as a central institution, but you also have all kinds of other very interesting institutions around it that are pretty big, Hayward, Serpentine, Whitechapel and so on. Of course, in this region BALTIC is the first institution, but hopefully this will generate lots of other interests.

JAMES LINGWOOD:

I think there is a danger with institutions of that scale and this new generation of institutions, particularly when it comes to commissioning, which is to do with gigantism in a way. There's a sense in which the spaces demand a kind of response, which is inappropriate to the languages of those artists you are bringing in to it. I'm afraid today there's a pretty good example of that problem which has just opened at Tate Britain, which reminded me of how unsuccessful most of the other commissions in those Duveen Galleries at the Tate have been. I think probably with the exception of the two artists who I recall sticking very close to the ground: one was Richard Long and the other was Richard Serra, so they didn't actually try and deal with the scale of the building, they kept horizontal. And I think the same problem will be apparent when the new Tate opens. You can never pre-judge a work from maquettes – the space is going to be awesome, it is like entering a cathedral and they've invited Louise Bourgeois to make the opening commission. And Louise Bourgeois never leaves New York now, so she's worked entirely from photos with assistants and is going to build some very large towers in this building. And they feel to me like very large drawings blown up in space. I mean, her work is exquisite on paper and sometimes with certain plays of material, as a kind of continuation of the Surrealist project, but blown up to thirty metres or whatever the size is.., I have anxieties. I do think that institutions with that kind of space and also the financial muscle to do that, have to be very careful about what they do.

SUNE NORDGREN:

I really agree and I'm really happy we don't have that entrance at BALTIC. When you enter the BALTIC you enter through the Riverside Building with the café and bookshop etc. and when you enter the building itself, you enter to a white cube which is not more that 250 square metres.

It's a very beautiful gallery with a slate floor and white walls. It can be used for absolutely anything. But it's quite an intimate space. The big spaces are further up in the building. And the five spaces are all very different from each other so you never have this monumental hall. The high art gallery as we call it – it's a nice double meaning – is quite high, eight and a half metres to the ceiling, but it still has a human scale and material inside, so it's not this enormous scale...

PROF. JOHN MILNER:

You've been closely involved in designing this space without quite knowing what's going to go in it? James has been talking about some of the traps that can arise out of working backwards from the space to what will look good in there or what will challenge the space. Obviously there is, in that, a tuning in to what might go into a particular space. Artangel does this one way with extraordinary spaces and places. Very often you have on board all the associations of grand galleries and dealing with the public in a different way. So, this idea of the curator as a creative person, one can very much see moving into the spotlight in both of those cases. You were quite careful to say that you interfere only in the sense that...

JAMES LINGWOOD:

I think the curator or the producer is a creative person, moderately creative, in the sense that my work, whether it's in the museum context or outside, is one of close collaboration. But actually being an editor for a novelist is creative work and highly respected by the novelists, and could as much as cut in half the manuscript they've delivered, but nonetheless, the relationship between the two is fairly clear. I think it's important the curator understands their position in the foodchain, let's say.

PROF. JOHN MILNER:

You were wondering whether the various roles one might have conventionally isolated in the artworld combine? That of critic, that of curator...does the audience want to come in here?

QUESTION:

I'd like to comment from an artist's perspective to link this point to what Sune & James were saying about the dangers of artists making things too big under the pressures of presentation in these enormously imposing spaces. Surely it's up to the artists to say, 'no way, you're giving me this big space and I'm going to do small work or use part of the space'. And surely this gigantism is being encouraged by the way curators are working with artists. If they are editors then they could step in at that stage and say 'Hey, let's have a talk. I mean, you don't have to go big'. Do you see what I'm saying? There isn't that critical editing happening anymore it seems to me, with curators. Both the curators and the artists are relinquishing part of their critical role.

JAMES LINGWOOD:

I think, unfortunately, a lot of curators, particularly those that have worked within institutions for a long period of time, have relatively little experience of that direct editorial relationship. The relationship then has a danger of becoming rather fearful: fearful of broaching certain questions.

And that's where the problems arise. These institutions will, I think, learn pretty quickly to circumnavigate some of those problems and I suspect some of the most intelligent responses to those vast spaces will be comparatively discreet, or quite ludic in a way, rather than monumental.

SUNE NORDGREN:

My experience of Nancy Spero was very good, because she was offered this space, which is ten metres to the ceiling, about eight hundred square metres and she printed a band around the four walls and nothing else.
It was completely beautiful and occupied the complete space. So, being monumental is very much about the content of the work and not only the scale of it.

PROF. JOHN MILNER:

There's another role that comes to mind in this context, and that is patron. When you're commissioning work this is inevitably part of the story isn't it? Does anyone here want to raise any issues about the patronage role, and commissioning a work? I mean, there are artists present who may wonder how it is possible to approach Artangel or the BALTIC for example. You have before you two people who say they're really pliant, they are editors but they're not the prime movers in the creative process. Do people feel that there is a kind of power here, of the patron?

SUNE NORDGREN:

For me, the relation, talking about an 'editor' – I like that very much because I was an editor – there's no use having curators if they're not a part of the creative process. Then you just have a bunch of very good assistants following the artist's tail and trying to please them as much as possible. I mean, most of the artists that you work with have a vision and it's your work to try to come as close as possible to this vision with the means that you have in the gallery, in the budget etc. You could say that you follow the artist, but at the same time there will always be compromises. And the compromising and the fights are of course a part of the creative process.

That's why you have a curator. But you should never forget the inner seed....

QUESTION:

How do you go about selecting artists? Do you personally 'hand pick' or is there a way that they can approach you? Is it their reputation? You have the power to hand pick and choose who you want.

SUNE NORDGREN:

If I think back to my practice – about twenty five years back – both as a book publisher, but also as a curator, I think that most of the works that have come to a good result have been artists that I've approached myself. Fewer have been where the artist came with a full synopsis for something.

Because it's a choice that you make. The artists that you choose, that you really want to work with, makes for a special relationship from the start.

QUESTION:

So is that you as an individual or as a panel?

SUNE NORDGREN:

Well, it was very much me as an individual. I saw myself very much as a dictator (audience laughter) and I used to justify it because I had a contract – it's the same with BALTIC – for five years. After me there will be another subject, another person. So, if I have five years, of course

I would like to realise some of my dream projects. But at the same time, or course you have a responsibility...

QUESTION:

It's also a very powerful position...

SUNE NORDGREN:

Of course. A very powerful position. That's why you should use it in a clever way. Of course you will always be criticised and in the BALTIC there will be a curatorial team, and ideas will come from this team as well as from outside, from artists, and we will all agree on something. But I think it's very difficult if you just try to do a programme based on what everyone wants and try to please everyone. That's not really a challenge: not for you, not for the staff.

QUESTION (TO SUNE NORDGREN):

Are you under pressure to have 'big name' artists? This place has got to cut ice on the international art scene, so you've got to have some 'big names'. In your slides, you showed a lot of well-known names who have been shown in institutions all over the world. Will it be something rather like that at the BALTIC?

SUNE NORDGREN:

Of course I did lots of other things also with both regional artists and Swedish artists, that I didn't show and they were also very successful. I think that at the BALTIC it's important to have a combination of both, because, even if you have a very famous artist, as you say, I don't think this artist's name will attract the main public for BALTIC. So, first of all you need to create a kind of trust and confidence in the place itself.

It's also a need to be recognised in the international art world....

PROF. JOHN MILNER:

So you're involved in competition yourself in a way.

SUNE NORDGREN:

Of course, yes.

PROF. JOHN MILNER:

But both of these points illustrate that any selection deselects most of the candidates, so there is an element of patronage there. I'm not saying this is wrong. I'm just intrigued to see what the mechanics of it are.

QUESTION:

But it's authorship as well. Both presentations that you've given tell us stories about what we've seen and we get a kind of history and level of anecdote that we might not get from the artist. And (to James Lingwood) your point about the relationship between an editor and an author, if one takes the example of John Clare and John Taylor, his editor, he more or less re-wrote John Clare's poems to suit his audience. He was a medium in a very real, strong sense, and a kind of an author. So it (curating) is a creative act and it is an act of authorship isn't it? And there should be some way of talking about that?

PROF. JOHN MILNER:

Well I think a lot of the exhibitions we glimpsed in the brief surveys, were that, they were events. Rather than a retro-spective monographic or historical assemblage of material, you were enabling the events to occur. So this is very different from collecting objects and it's a different kind of relationship really.

JAMES LINGWOOD:

I think this is an interesting area. I try to kind of calibrate the relationship that I see myself having with certain artists and of course it's more authorial in some cases than others, as an editor's would be, and that relates somehow to the personal relationship that you build up with an artist. I don't want to be in denial about my creativity or indeed my powers of patronage. But at the same time I don't see the two as being on the same level and I don't want to confuse my contribution to the genesis of a project with what the artist brings to it. I think one of the key instinctive skills that a commissioning producer has, is knowing when to step back from the creative process. Basically the creative process is opaque and it's volatile and it's unpredictable. Where a lot of commissions fall flat is when the people involved demand transparency and demand knowing what's going on at the wrong time. So, I think one develops a kind of distinctive feel for the particular chemistry of the particular process and sometimes you get it better than other times. There is a need for a more creative authorial role and sometimes there's a need to really keep your distance.

QUESTION:

That's one of the things that's interesting. It took a historian to unravel the fact, as I understand it, that John Taylor had done so much to John Clare's poems. That's the sort of thing you're talking about isn't it, it's often not seen?

SUNE NORDGREN:

I think that's another part. This has to do with the education doesn't it?

What you meet very often in institutions, after the work is created, you want to have as many visitors as possible, because there is a budget to keep and so on. And the education comes in and tries to popularise the artists' work. Sometimes I have the feeling that some curators want to include the education part already in the creative process, which is really dangerous, because then you get lost; you lose this inner seed of the work, which you should never touch. That's the main problem with lots of museums today. Museum education is really important but everything starts with the art.

(Response to an audience question on the issue of collecting)

SUNE NORDGREN:

There is already an institution in this region that has the responsibility of collecting contemporary artworks, and I don't want to interfere with that institution. If they have a lousy budget for acquisitions, that's another question, but the responsibility is already with another institution. I wanted very much that the artworks created in or commissioned by the BALTIC shouldn't look....'could you make it a bit smaller so it will fit in our lift?' You shouldn't have those kinds of considerations when you work with an artist. So that's how it (referring to his article in Newsletter No. 7) started, but it's very ambiguous because my article ends with 'we should of course have some documentation of it'. I call it a kind of 'collective memory'. There will be some kind of collection at the BALTIC.

PROF. JOHN MILNER:

But of objects?

SUNE NORDGREN:

Well, sometimes you can't collect the object…so then you collect documentation.

JAMES LINGWOOD:

Certainly at Artangel we don't feel we own the commissioning process, but we feel that we share it. At a certain point there may or may not be something that can endure in one form or another. It could be a sculpture which is bought by a museum, at which point we would wish to reclaim the fabrication costs. I mean actually, without having thought about this too much, I think if you take an overview of the development of the visual arts in England, it's extremely important that major collections of contemporary art are generated beyond what the Tate Gallery are doing, because it's a phenomenal organisation with the greatest powers of patronage and acquisition that we have. But if it becomes too totalising, there are inherent dangers. So I'm not saying to Sune here and now the BALTIC should collect. But out of this extraordinary investment in new infrastructure around Britain, if none of those institutions form collections, I think it'll be a great shame and it does seem to me that the BALTIC is perhaps one of those in a position to take that on. And it doesn't need to be a collection that tries to be representative of movements or developments or whatever, but it can start from now and build from there.

PROF. JOHN MILNER:

Did you regret – as a kind of owner – the loss of the 'House' (by Rachel Whiteread)?

JAMES LINGWOOD:

No, I think it was appropriate.

PROF. JOHN MILNER:

And as you say, it does live on in some way.

JAMES LINGWOOD:

Its limited life became part of its conceptual development.
Of course there were debates about its prolongation
which were interesting to participate in, and I regret that it
didn't have a longer life, simply because there was an
enormous potential audience. Vast numbers of people saw
it but even more probably would have got to see it. But
also, even after eighty days, it was beginning to look not
so good: as it got sprayed with graffiti and it started to
lose its 'otherness' as a presence and started to become
more like a derelict house.

PROF. JOHN MILNER:

Once you raised the issue of ownership and collecting
and that kind of thing, it's perhaps possible to see a little
more about the previous question, about pressures to be
international in your scope, view and ambition, or national
and does this have any conflict with the local population?

SUNE NORDGREN:

Not really. I mean art has nothing to do with geography.
Art has to do with quality.

PROF. JOHN MILNER:

Spoken like a Swede, if I may say. But it's different isn't it....

SUNE NORDGREN:

Yes, England is different, I've started to notice that!
But anyway, I mean we have to work on all these levels.
And we know that the main public for an art centre in
Gateshead will be a local and regional public – we're about

two million people here around Tyne and Wear. The main public for BALTIC has to come out of those two million people and from Scotland of course.

We might be able to attract a few Londoners as well!

But that's one level. The other is the national level, and then you have the international level. The international level is very few in terms of numbers of people, but at the same time, what we are doing is justified by those people. And even the local public here, what they hear and read about the BALTIC...to be really honest, the whole place will be justified by people far away from here. That's the truth. Having said that, in the five spaces we have and with the budget we have, this programme and these possibilities we have of generating things here, I strongly believe that very much of it will be generated by regional and national artists.

QUESTION:

I feel a bit critical about the way that...international institutions...like the Guggenheim, all around the world show the same kind of work in the same kind of way.

SUNE NORDGREN:

Most of these institutions luckily have very big collections so they can fill most of their space from their collection. Places like Bilbao, which hasn't really got a very good collection, it's a 'deselection' of the Guggenheim, New York, it's like a temporary space for Guggenheim, New York. And that's problematic, when you get those kinds of institutions everywhere. There was an idea in England, not long ago, of having Tate's everywhere, it started with Tate Liverpool and then there was St. Ives and they wanted to have more and more Tate's everywhere. There are four now and that's fair enough, it's good. (To questioner) But I don't agree with you that they show the same exhibitions...

QUESTION:

They show the same names.

SUNE NORDGREN:

They do, but the amount of names has grown if you look back about fifteen years. If you look back at the new museum boom in Germany in the mid-80s, it was exactly the same. They were competing and building these new cathedrals all around in Germany and they had the same artists, there was always a Joseph Beuys in the entrance and so on. But when you visit them now, they are much more diverse. I think that the international scene is growing rapidly now. Not in Britain unfortunately, because the problem in Britain and England is that you have been very successful in the last twenty years with all your artists, which means that you have been justified by the international scene. The British artists are so interesting that you don't need to show anyone else. Which means that it's been – I don't know if James agrees – less inter-national. There have been less big international shows in London than there have been in other capitals around the world. In lots of those international biennials and lots of the big international museums around the world, you see an expansion, with African artists, Asian artists, Latin American artists, Scandinavian artists, so I think that the international scene has grown rapidly in the last five – six years. But you don't see it here, yet. You will.

PROF. JOHN MILNER (TO JAMES LINGWOOD):

It's amazing that you can thrive and survive, without a colos-sal cathedral. It seems extraordinary there should be this choice of having a colossal cathedral and not, in a way…

JAMES LINGWOOD:

Well, I think if we do more than survive it's probably because we don't have one. A lot of the bigger institutions historically have been like icebergs: the vast majority of their activities and their holdings have been beneath the threshold of visibility, with the tip of it above. What we've tried to do, is to invert the iceberg. We're very small beneath the water so that the majority of our resources – which is about money because we don't have much – in terms of energy and in terms of attention, are above the surface. We have grown over the last three or four years to the extent that I feel uncomfortable with that even. You do the best work in this area I think when you really are flexible and you can sort of reinvent yourself all the time. I just wanted to come back to this question of how conspiratorial the international art world is. You know, it appears to be so but actually, it's populated by idiosyncratic, wilful and quite individualistic people. I think if you take a broad overview, it's not quite as conventional as you might suggest. I think the difficulties for a lot of organisations – and this is something that Sune will have to address – is keeping the whole thing afloat, keeping the whole thing economically buoyant or whatever. And insufficient time is available for what you call 'field research' – actually getting out there and trying to get beyond that mediated area where the names come up, to go beyond that. I'm not sure that we do that enough either but it's something we attempt to carve out time to do.

QUESTION:

That's one of the things I was thinking about. You're picking names because you've seen their work before, probably in the big galleries. So do you ever go 'underground' so to speak, to visit artists in their studios? How do you go about that?

SUNE NORDGREN:

Of course. I think it's the most important part of the practice: to go and see artists in their studios.

That's what I'm trying to do as well and it will be part of the BALTIC practice once we're open. For the moment we're working on a pre-opening programme, which is trying to draw attention to the development itself and so on. But it's another thing once we're open and we have all these facilities – digital suites, exhibition spaces and so on – to work with. No, you constantly do it and when you visit somewhere, you always make appointments with artists to go and see their studios.

QUESTION:

So how do you go about that? Do you go to slide indexes?

SUNE NORDGREN:

No. They're never updated enough! Although Axis, as you know, is one which seems to be more rapidly updated and relevant.

PROF. JOHN MILNER:

There are lots of artists here today of course. What does the problem look like from the artists' point of view? Or are there other questions around this: how do you gain access to, how do you know that people are trying to look for you? How do you make this link?

QUESTION:

That's why I was asking. There are lots of people who are working in certain ways and there is a very particular type of work that is being shown. And there's a type of work that is not being shown but it's going on.

JAMES LINGWOOD:

What types of work are not being shown? Yours?
(audience laughter)

QUESTION:

No, I mean people who are perhaps in the craft area,
maybe they're carving or they're doing something in a
traditional fashion. They often see themselves very much
on the periphery...but they are out there doing it.

JAMES LINGWOOD:

I think that's true. Carving's having a bad time...(audience
laughter)

QUESTION:

But that sort of discipline. And painting in any sort of traditional sense. There are plenty of people doing it. A lot of
people doing it very badly as well.

SUNE NORDGREN:

But also lots of lousy video art. It's not just a matter of
medium is it? It's a matter of quality.

QUESTION:

Yes, very much. I think it's got a lot to do with what's
happening in art colleges: there isn't anyone teaching
these things.

QUESTION:

I think one of the things you are trying to refer to is the
question of accountability. I mean who are the publicly
funded arts bodies in each country accountable to in the
end? James mentioned it to a certain degree (although)

they're not under the same pressure of putting 'bums on seats' as maybe other institutions are, but of course there is a question of accountability.

But surely that is the question that everyone is really asking: If the spaces, institutions, operate as a filter system? Of course there's nothing to prevent artists from creating their own public situations and in fact that was how all this started off, if you want to go back to the beginning of the film. If there's a relationship between what gets shown, just to generalise, at the sort of level that we're seeing today, and some other institutions, such as the market, then I think people should be very frank about that, because there is. And that is why people in the audience are complaining that the same artists circulate all the time. The actual filter system happens to be the market. How that intersects with notions of public accountability is very interesting and I personally would be fascinated to hear both of your comments on that.

JAMES LINGWOOD:

Well, I think that the market is not purely and simply the validating mechanism; I don't even think you're suggesting that entirely. The market happens to be extremely fleet of foot and capable of absorbing what is going on in the artworld and commodifying or repackaging it in a way.

We certainly acknowledge that the market is one of the forces in the magnetic field in which we are working but I certainly don't think it's necessarily the strongest or the primary force.

SUNE NORDGREN:

What we have shown in the slides tonight, gives, in one way the wrong impression, at least of my practice.

Because, what we are talking about – commissions and things – are very often spectacular events. I mean the Anish Kapoor was up for eight weeks and then it was down again. But when I look back, at least every second exhibition I have made in my curatorial practice has been 'flat' things on the wall: photography, painting. Because that's one of the main streams of the practice and has always been. I agree that perhaps one of those 'spectacular' event entails more…the media in this country is so concentrated in London and to attract the media you need to be spectacular. It's very difficult to be spectacular in painting for the moment, but I think you can.

PROF. JOHN MILNER:

Does it exist still, the Anish Kapoor (installation)?

SUNE NORDGREN:

It exists. It's stored but it is unlikely to be shown again.

QUESTION:

With the exhibitions at the BALTIC, how will you go about noticing the difference between when you're commissioning work going on around you and work that's brought within? When it's around, it will be generated by the uniqueness of the BALTIC, and will be able to take many different forms and be interpreted in many different ways. But surely when it's taken into the BALTIC, into this constant 'white cube' space, it will come together with everything else, every other white cube space…

SUNE NORDGREN:

It's just one of the five galleries which is a white cube….

QUESTION:

They're still constant spaces....

SUNE NORDGREN:

Yes, that's true. They're quite big and quite flexible so you change them around. But it will still be an institution where you bring in the art. That's true. There are also working spaces inside BALTIC, which is very important. There will be at least three artists always working inside BALTIC in the different artists' workspaces and studios. But what I'm also hoping for is that there will be something similar here to Iaspis, the artist' studio programme I created in Stockholm, where I always mixed local, national and international artists in the eleven studios. I'm hoping for something similar here in Newcastle and there are already discussions going on.

QUESTION:

One of the interesting things about having conversations with artists is this relationship with audience. There were a number of Artangel projects, Stephen Balkenol or Rachel Whiteread, that actually worked with the way an audience builds up for that project...almost through rumour. And the way that say Artangel might work allows things to happen and I think those kinds of opportunities are also available up here. It's an interesting area: things can be grounded and associated with, say, BALTIC but actually happen elsewhere.

QUESTION:

What about the link to the place, the Baltic countries....you talked about the Swedish floor...
(audience laughter)

SUNE NORDGREN:

I'm sorry it said BALTIC on the building when I arrived here, I couldn't do anything about it. What I'm hoping for, is that it will be shortened down even further to just 'B.'(B.dot). But it is BALTIC and I can't do anything about it for the moment. There is a museum in Denmark called Louisiana, and it works quite well. (audience laughter)

PROF. JOHN MILNER:

The other side of that question was about the links across the North Sea. Is this something that you want to keep?

SUNE NORDGREN:

Not necessarily. I know there a quite a few interesting Scandinavian artists and some of them have been shown here in Britain already, and of course there will be opportunities for that. But it's not necessarily something I'm looking for specifically.

PROF. JOHN MILNER:

This is the first in a series of discussions and we've only just cracked open one or two issues. We have other debates with curators of very different kinds to look forward to.

Thanks to speakers and audience applause.

THE PRODUCERS:
CONTEMPORARY CURATORS
IN CONVERSATION

8TH JUNE 2000, UNIVERSITY OF NEWCASTLE,
DEPARTMENT OF FINE ART.

CLIVE PHILLPOT AND MATTHEW HIGGS
IN CONVERSATION
CHAIRED BY SUNE NORDGREN

SUSAN HILLER:

Thank you all for coming on what is rather an unusual day
to be having a major event like this. Just to introduce
myself briefly, I'm Susan Hiller and I'd like to welcome you
on behalf of the Department of Fine Art, University of
Newcastle and the BALTIC Centre for Contemporary Art
to the second in the series of curatorial discussions
between distinguished curators. Today's session will be
chaired by Sune Nordgren, Director of the BALTIC Centre

for Contemporary Art, well known to most of you I'm sure. Our two speakers are very interesting in their differences and in their similarities. In fact all three of the people sitting at the table have been very involved in that field of art which has come to be known as artists' books and perhaps some of their interests will come out in discussion. Clive Phillpot is famous for having formed some of the best artists' books libraries of the 60s and 70s, first at Chelsea College of Arts and then as Director of the Library at the Museum of Modern Art in New York. He is currently Librarian of the Visual Arts department of the British Council. Clive is also known as a writer of catalogues and essays and as the curator and organiser of some extremely interesting exhibitions, for example, 'Networking' in 1996, which featured the work of Ray Johnson, Mike Kelly, David Hockney, among others. He's particularly interested in counter-cultural manifestations within art, particularly the use of ephemera, such as in artists' books and correspondence art or mail art. But perhaps he is best known at the moment as the co-curator of the very large and very exciting exhibition of British conceptual work of the 60s and 70s held at the Whitechapel Art Gallery, called 'Live in Your Head'.

Matthew Higgs originally trained as a fine artist in the painting department of what was then called Newcastle Polytechnic in the late 80s and he now defines his practice as being almost equally divided between curating, writing, publishing, making his own work and teaching. He's recently been appointed as Associate Director of Exhibitions at the ICA in London. He's written quite a few unusual publications, including something called the Tate Gallery Celebrity List and has curated a number of excitingly controversial exhibitions and has also worked as visiting curator of artists' books for Bookworks in London. At the moment he's working on a large exhibition, interestingly enough also to be held at the Whitechapel Art Gallery in September ('Protest and Survive') which will

include the work of artists such as Dan Graham, Jo
Spence, Richard Hamilton, the Hackney flashers, Jeremy
Deller and so forth. I'll turn over to the speakers now.

SUNE NORDGREN:

Thank you Susan. We'd like to do it a similar way to the
last time, so the two combatants here, the two speakers,
will do a presentation about their work. We've limited it to
fifteen minutes to make time for discussion between the
two and some questions from you of course. So, I would
like to ask Clive Phillpot to start his presentation.

CLIVE PHILLPOT:

In April last year, 1999, I was approached by Andrea
Tarsia, Curator at the Whitechapel Art Gallery to talk
about the possibility of working on an exhibition at the
Whitechapel. We met, and he said that they were doing
this show at the Whitechapel in February 2000, something
to do with British conceptualism in the 60s and 70s. They
were thinking of calling it 'Live in Your Head', and had
started with about a dozen or so artists who might be
included, now expanded by Andrea to about fifty. I
thought, 'Wow, it's scheduled for February and we're only
talking now?'

It seemed like they needed someone to work with
Andrea, who had perhaps witnessed some of the contemporary events, who might be an advisor, or, as I soon
learned, actually co-curator of the exhibition and co-editor
of the catalogue. So, it seemed like it was my job in a way
to research what might be in there and who might be in
there, from my own experience. So, in a slow kind of way,
I began to look through the records of what I thought
were the seminal shows. On reflection this was a strategy
that might not have been the best way, certainly not the
only way to approach the period, but it did seem to me
that one had to reprise the history for another generation,

and one way that we found out about it was to look at particular shows that had formed opinion and attitudes. In addition, the title that had been given to my friend Andrea, 'Live in Your Head', was itself part of the title of an important international exhibition of the time: 'When Attitudes Become Form.'

'When Attitudes Become Form', organised by Harald Szeeman, was shown in Bern early in 1969 and then brought to the ICA in London that summer, where a few extra works were added by Charles Harrison. This was one of the first exhibitions in Britain to show that something else was happening beyond certain kinds of formalism and minimalism; it was somewhat sculptural. The catalogue had included the phrase 'Live In Your Head', and this was the origin of the slogan, the main title, for the Whitechapel show. But we also inherited a subtitle that gave me problems: it talked about British conceptual and experimental art between whatever dates we had at that point, in the sixties and seventies.

I really didn't want to deal with British conceptual art as such, because, Art-Language aside, conceptual art seemed to me to be a particular historical moment that was something to do with New York in the late sixties, and people like Kosuth and Barry and Huebler and Weiner. Therefore it seemed that to restrict ourselves to conceptualism in England was very weird when essential elements of this happened in New York – and other places, of course. So I argued that the scope should be not quite as stark as 'conceptual and experimental art', that perhaps just 'concept and experiment' would be a better way into the new developments – though perhaps I should have gone further still. Similarly, I also objected to the word 'British' because this was such a time of interaction, travelling; with many of the people who contributed to the scene passing through or just arriving from other countries. The Beau Geste collective in Devon epitomised this, as did the Destruction in Art Symposium. So we used 'in Britain' which I thought was reasonable. (There have been several great international shows, 'Out of Actions', for example, that inevitably included only a sprinkling of artists who had worked in Britain. It seemed to me that it was a good time to reveal the depth of experiment and change in Britain at that time.) I mention all this, because if you're interested in the curating process, you'll see that this was all very fluid. In a way I had been presented with a blueprint that I felt I had to modify. I hadn't come along with a fresh idea, I had to work with what I was given. Another thing, if we had focused on about ten or twenty artists, say, it seemed to me the show would have been totally restrictive and wouldn't have added up to a useful overview of the diverse activities that were happening in Britain during a very vital time. Finally, it also seemed appropriate to me to push the dates, from '66 to '74, say, to '65 on the one hand and to '75 on the other, both to make the time period more arbitrary and to de-emphasise that something crucial happened in 1966, which is not untrue, and that everything followed from this. Rather we should take a decade and say what happened in this particular slice of time. It more or less embraces the phase of experiment, for a lot of things happened between '66 and '73, though some relevant things also happened before '65.

After my initial meeting with Andrea Tarsia I spent about a month doing research on the period of the sixties and early seventies. I developed a list that rose to about 130 artists. There were one or two crucial sources that seemed to sum up what had been happening here in that period: one was the sort of official exhibition 'The New Art' at the Hayward Gallery in 1972, whilst another, almost simultaneous and produced in reaction to it was 'A Survey of the Avant-Garde in Britain', held at Gallery House. These two surveys were practically antithetical, but to a degree expressed what had gone on in the years up to 1972. So I went through the catalogues and reminded myself who was in there, and began to amplify my list. There was also an exhibition in New York that was documented in an issue of 'Studio International' magazine in 1971 called 'The British Avant Garde'. There were some artists in that show that I hadn't heard of since that date, or only rarely, so it became very interesting for me to add them to my list and try to find out what had happened to them; where they might be. (It was the cause of some regret for everyone in the show, including myself, that we could only show a snapshot of what was happening between '65 and '75 – a lot of the people in the show have done great work since then. We talked of a follow-up show of the same artists in another decade.)

As well as these exhibitions and their catalogues, I looked at other sources for the names of artists who had worked in Britain at that time. One such was 'Fluxshoe' published by Beau Geste Press in 1972. This documented the international cast of characters who were involved in a show that travelled round the country in '72 and '73. Another was the book of the 'Wall Show' at the Lisson Gallery in '71. Then there was the Seth Siegelaub exhibition catalogues of 1969 and those of the New York exhibitions of 1970: 'Information' at MoMA and 'Conceptual Art and Conceptual Aspects' at the New York Cultural Centre. I also went through Lucy Lippard's book 'Six Years' and so on. And I musn't forget 'Studio International' and 'Art and Artists'.

Ultimately, it was clear that 130 artists were too many for the exhibition, so after Andrea and I had merged our lists, various artists were regretfully excluded. Some excluded themselves. One artist didn't want to be in the show; one or two others didn't keep in touch. The catalogue of 'Live in Your Head' tells you who finally constituted the show.

Let me now show you slides of the installations as if you were strolling through the exhibition. I should add that Andrea and I split responsibility for working with the various artists in the show between us, so not only will my account be subjective, but I know more about securing some pieces than others. (shows slides)

In the lobby of the Whitechapel gallery we displayed the catalogue which was designed in four colours. Well, it wasn't designed in four colours, we simply couldn't decide what colour the cover should be. One thing I really wanted to do was to do was to include John & Yoko's 'War is Over!' billboard, that was originally shown near Piccadilly in 1969. We got permission to recreate it, and originally wanted to show it outside, at the top of the building facing out into the street, but in the end had to have it done in the gallery lobby by sign painters at much less cost than putting scaffolding up in front of the building. That was one of the practical and financial problems we ran into. Also in the lobby was a sort of appendix to the show, a case with artists' books. Because of my history with artists' books I didn't even suggest this, it was Andrea who said that perhaps we should put some books in. Because of the space constraints, this was in the end just a gesture towards the fact that books were a very important new medium for artists. But it seemed important to me to put magazines in the main part of the exhibition in order to reveal a collaboration between artists and the fact that magazines often say more about group manifestations than other kinds of material. There were some important magazines exhibited, notably 'Art and Language', but also something like 'Schmuck', which brought together the more Fluxus performance side of things.

You get your first glimpse of the main gallery from the lobby. I don't always like the way the Whitechapel is laid out whereby you first walk up to a barrier of an inside wall. I wanted a vista that would allow you to see the whole space. At one time we had a vista all the way through to the far wall, but we finally had to build some rooms at the back to show movies and video, so the vista was shortened. But it was still inviting and revealed the space quite well. The ground floor gallery is a beautiful space. Once you were in the gallery, right in front of you as you came in was a pile of oranges, 'Pyramid (Soul City)', a work by Roelof Louw dating back to 1967, to the time when post-Caro sculpture was moving in very interesting directions in London, with various new venues for showing large and ambitious works and for experimentation. He did something quite remarkable which was to build up this form, this pile of oranges, then as people came in he allowed them to take oranges away with them. Our idea was that this would be right in the middle of the gallery as you came in. There were all sorts of potential problems about whether the oranges would roll about, people would fall over, and so on, but in the end it was not a problem in that respect. The pyramid simply diminished as people passed through, though a lot of people thought it shouldn't be touched, whilst others thought they were being very daring in taking an orange.

To the right of the oranges was the only painting in the show, Bob Law's 'Mr Paranoia'. Indeed 'Pyramid' was really the only sculpture in the show. I felt that this was something we should demonstrate: that something other than painting and sculpture was happening in Britain at this time. So here was a painting that was somewhat empty. It's like the end of painting. The artist said his pictures were just a step away from conceptual art in the head. The vanishing pyramid was like the end of sculpture. And from here we move into what was new.

On the other side of the entrance was a piece called 'Women and Work': I really wanted this in the show. It was a collaboration between Margaret Harrison, Kay Hunt and Mary Kelly. We couldn't find it. I couldn't even track down Kay Hunt. I eventually found out where she was from a curator in Canada, via e-mail. The curator had shown the work in Canada as part of a Mary Kelly show and the very same piece was back in England on show at the Leeds City Art Gallery. But it was kind of appropriated, as if it was just part of Mary Kelly's oeuvre, so I was very keen, as were the other artists, to show this as a collaborative political work that came right out of the period of the early 70s. Eventually with the help of the people at Leeds and the consent of Mary Kelly, we were able to place a substantial part of the combined work of Margaret Harrison, Kay Fido (as she is now known) and Mary Kelly before the public.

The full version of 'Women and Work' had originally been one whole exhibition. 'Live in Your Head' also included several abridged one-person shows from the 60s and 70s, including former solo shows by Robin Crozier, Susan Hiller, Tony Rickaby and Conrad Atkinson.

The next piece one came to was essential to the exhibition: John Latham's 'Still and Chew: Art and Culture'. This came from the collection of the Museum of Modern Art in New York, where I used to work, but this year they're showing nearly the whole collection and not lending very much so it was really difficult to get this piece although it was not going to be shown there until the Fall of 2000. It cost us an arm and a leg to get it. There are very few loans from overseas in the show, but this seemed to be essential and when the courier who brought it here arrived, she said, 'it's very pleasing for me to be able to repatriate things from time to time'. But it's now back in New York. This seemed to be absolutely seminal: Latham at that time, and before '65, was extremely important in establishing a different kind of art in this country. And his friends' chewing and spitting out of Clement Greenberg's 'Art and Culture' to make a new culture was punningly symbolic of this new beginning.

Another person I was keen to get in here, someone who taught across the river at Sunderland for a long time, Robin Crozier. This wonderful piece, 'Portrait of Robin Crozier' happened because he wrote to over a hundred people around the world, many of whom were classic figures in mail art, asking them to send him portraits of himself. Since most of them had never met him, the results were very diverse. This work was also a trojan horse which enabled me to get some artists from overseas into the show, artists such as Ray Johnson, Robert Filious, Ben Vautier, Mieko Shiomi, Davi Det Hompson, Anna Banana, and many more. The large number of people participating included Bill Coldstream, then Head of the Slade, rather unwittingly, as well as artists also included elsewhere in 'Live in Your Head'.

At the centre of the main gallery was Art and Language's 'Index 01' of 1972. When I was thinking about how they might be represented, there were two pieces I particularly wanted in. One is a map of a thirty six square mile area of the Pacific Ocean where there's no land masses – the map is actually completely vacant. Then another piece, seven or eight years later, which seems on the surface very similar, about a kind of negative depiction. But the guys who are Art and Language shifted from Michael Baldwin and Terry Atkinson, who did the first piece, to Michael Baldwin and Mel Ramsden who did the second. So these two pieces show Art and Language having both consistency and difference as they changed their personnel. In fact I called Terry Atkinson first to get his reading on showing the changing group but he suggested I call Michael Baldwin. This led to a meeting in the country at which Michael, Mel, Charles Harrison and I discussed the choice of a major work that might represent most of the artists and others who were involved with Art and Language at that time. Hence the choice of an 'Index'. Originally we planned to show 'Index 02', but due to international incidents ultimately showed 'Index 01' which is a literal index of the work of the group to 1972, and is, ironically, the piece that spurred Terry Atkinson's departure from Art & Language.

As I said, Andrea and I divided the artists between ourselves, so that ultimately we each took responsibility for thirty-odd artists. Andrea introduced the idea of including visual poetry, which I'm fascinated with and care about a lot. In this case, he left me to decide who we should have, while I left him to decide which film makers should be included. In the end I settled on four artists: Bob Cobbing, dom sylvester houédard, Henri Chopin and Tom Edmonds. Tom Edmonds died when he was about twenty seven– leaving behind a few beautiful works. Strangely enough, the only other person in the show who had already died was the monk dom sylvester houédard. Everybody else was alive and pretty well.

Bob Cobbing was a key figure of the time. He managed a bookshop called Better Books across the road from St Martins School of Art, when St Martins was very lively, with students like Gilbert and George, Bruce Mclean, Richard Long, Barry Flanagan, some of whom got involved in this place which housed performance, film, readings etc. as well as avant-garde publications. We both went to see Bob and discussed with him how we might show his work. He just said 'do what you like'. So, since I liked the idea of mega-graphics, we blew up nine of his visual poems and fixed them to the wall. His work is one example of mounted photocopies in the show. There are other photocopies such as 'Launching the Great Wall of China into Orbit…' by David Medalla, who also took a casual attitude to the presentation of his work. The big question to me was do these photocopies constitute the art or not? What is the validity of these things? It didn't seem to matter to the visitors.

Before I got into the planning with Andrea Tarsia I thought that it was possible that the show would be characterised by plenty of texts, with or without images. In the end I was surprised how few texts we included. We ended up with David Medalla's 'MMMMMMM…Manifesto', Gustave Metzger's 'Artists Engaged in Political Struggle' – about the art strike – and Keith Arnatt's 'Is it Possible for Me to do Nothing as my Contribution to this Exhibition?', three equally punchy but diverse pieces, ranging over the spectrum of the exhibition. These were all photocopies.

We also included Derek Boshier's 'Sixteen Situations' upstairs in the show, which some people found to be an odd inclusion. But it represented another thing about this period, that all definitions were breaking down and that although he had been characterised as a Pop artist and had been an abstract sculptor, he also produced this piece which seemed to me to be entirely in tune with works by other artists in the show. What he does is have this little minimal sculpture shown in various contexts, like in the palm of your hand or the middle of the universe. It's an entirely conceptual idea.

John Dugger's banner 'Chile Vencera' of 1974 is a piece I particularly wanted to include, in order to represent direct political actions by artists. Initially I tried to get the Artists Liberation Front banner which he did in 1971 with David Medalla, but he told me it had been stolen at Documenta in 1972, so I happily settled for his Chile banner. This was made for and used in Trafalgar Square at an anti-Pinochet rally after the death of Salvador Allende. The banner was so colourful, it was going to be hung on the ground floor at the far end, so you'd see it as you came in. But in the end, because we couldn't have these various cubicles for projections built in the upstairs gallery, they went downstairs, and we put the banner upstairs at the end of the vista. It worked fairly well.

I had better stop at this point in order to allow time for discussion.

(Audience Applause)

SUNE NORDGREN:

Thank you Clive. This show, which you have just been running through, is a very good example of how unpredictable the art public is. It was supposed to be a very 'specialist' show, and the Whitechapel had lots of problems with finding a sponsor for it, but it turned out to have 60,000 visitors. So, let's go on to Matthew.

MATTHEW HIGGS:

I grew up near Manchester in a small town called Chorley. Around the age of thirteen I started to write a music fanzine – this was in 1978 – and for me literature, ephemera, publishing, has always been there, since that age. I'm not really sure at the time what the motivation was to write a music fanzine. But I think it was an attempt to try to find a different level of engagement than what was being presented to me in a small town, which had very few opportunities for contact or networks beyond that. I guess my interest in contemporary art emerged simultaneously around this time, through bands like Throbbing Gristle, Cabaret Voltaire, particularly the bands that were on Factory Records in Manchester. (Slide) This is a photo of the band Joy Division taken in 1978 and I guess they formed everything I believe in. Everything I think about comes from my interest in Joy Division.

(Slide) This was the invitation card to an exhibition I had in London last year. I very recently started making work again. As was said, I went to the Polytechnic here. I left in '87 and I didn't make art for about five years after that experience. (audience laughter) I made work for a couple of years, then stopped again. It's only really in the last two years I've started making work again. This is me (slide) in the background of this photograph, with my hand on my mouth. The experience of doing a music fanzine has pretty much informed everything I do now. What struck me at the time, what was really quite astonishing, was that Joy Division – who I thought were really adults, though in reality they were twenty year olds – encouraged me as a person of some interest, they allowed me to go and watch them rehearse, they got me in to concerts, allowed me to interview them. It struck me as interesting that as a thirteen year old you could be taken seriously and your efforts could find an audience. Just doing a small circulation music fanzine at the time – maybe 200/300 issues – all of a sudden I found myself in correspondence with people all around the world. At that time my world consisted of a 100 mile radius. All of a sudden I was in contact with people in Belgium, the States, Germany – places I'd certainly never visited. It opened up an idea that it's possible to achieve something on a limited means or a limited scale.

(Slide) This is the kind of work I was making. My work has always been informed by text, by language. This was a piece called 'Total Despair'. It's the entire of Nabakov's novel 'Despair', front and back of each page, attached to the gallery wall in a grid. Every single line of the novel is crossed out very carefully in ink. So from a distance it still reads as a printed text, but in fact it's all been carefully erased with the exception of a single sentence on page 94 which reads 'ah me, what can there be more common-place than an impecunious artist? If some good soul would help me to arrange an exhibition, next day I'd be famous and rich'. At this time in London, round '91 and '92, ideas of success were very present. Ideas, percep-tions of success or the role of the artist, the function of the artist, was something I was interested in. I was looking towards earlier genre fictions, in this case Nabokov, but more particularly detective novels, to find earlier moments where there was this corrupted, base idea of the artist. (Slide) This was a small self-published book called 'Five Book pages'. It's taken from a Charles Willeford Novel: Charles Willeford is probably my favourite detective novel-ist. I guess he's associated with pulp detective writing, but it does his writing an injustice to call it pulp.

Throughout it (the novel) there's these statements. I graduated from a painting department, and I was interested in how these attitudes from the 1950s had a kind of currency now: 'I use painting as a substitute for love. All painters do, it's in their nature', 'Why wasn't I the one artist in a thousand who could make his living by painting?', 'All my life I only wanted to paint. There isn't any substitute for painting', and this is my favourite, 'Without art as an emotional outlet I turned to drinking as a substitute. I've been drinking ever since'. (Audience laughter).

So this was the kind of work I was making, but increasingly it was starting to manifest itself in other publications. The way that publications can be used to disseminate material still interests me a great deal and it's obviously something I encountered from that period. (Slide) This is a project for an American publication called 'Publicsfear'. I was really only looking at genre fiction at the time: this is from romantic fiction, Mills and Boon novels. It was a fourteen page project, just leaving a single sentence on each page. It's very funny when Mills and Boon use male artists as the romantic leads, because in detective fiction, and certainly Nabokov, the male artist is always perceived as this fucked-up loser. In the Mills and Boon novels they're always these Greek Adonis-like types and they're really super-confident. (explains plot of novel) On the last page of my piece there's just a single sentence, which says, 'she suspected he was itching to get his little chisel back to work' (laughter)…I would put 'big chisel' if I was a Mills and Boon writer.

There's lots of crossovers with the things that Clive was talking about: I've worked with quite a lot of the people who were in the 'Live in Your Head' exhibition, including Stephen Willats. (Slide) This is 'Control' Magazine, which he's been publishing since the early 60s. I really admire this magazine's irregularity. I think it's taken thirty four years to do sixteen issues. I think at one time he used to offer subscriptions, but it would be really painful waiting for it. (Next slide) This is a project that's ongoing for me. When I arrived in London, I had five years in a job in an ad agency and they used to get every single local newspaper in Britain every week. I used to go through every single one and cut out all the stories about how art was reported in local newspapers, once you're away from the metropolitan centre, once you're away from the broadsheets. This is how art manifested itself in local newspapers. What I love is you end up with headlines like 'art exhibition attracts visitors' (laughter). That's news!

I think one of the things art school does or can do, is it can temper your youthful enthusiasm for things. Certainly my teenage enthusiasm for things had been to some degree tempered by my experience at art school. Around '92 I was in London seeing an awful lot of interesting work, a lot of artists showing for the first time, and not necessarily people I knew. Like the fanzine which I always used as a kind of filter to allow me to have a conversation with a band. I was trying to think about starting that conversation again with these artists whose work I was seeing for the first time and started a small project called Imprint 93 which is still going on. It's obviously informed by the aesthetics and the ideology of Fluxus, and to some degree Mail Art, in that a lot of the projects are distributed by mail. I've never really graduated towards Mail Art as an activity in itself. Basically the invitation was for an artist to make anything they wanted to make, the only condition being that it be made very cheaply because the project is entirely self-financed, and remains so. It's always distributed for free. I think to date I've made seventy projects. It's much less regular now than it used to be but I'm going to revive it again.

(Slide) This was few years ago. It's just a general shot to give you an idea of some of the things I published, the general aesthetic or tone of these things. I think one reason that Imprint has become sort of culturally interesting – I don't really know where it sits – is that a number of the artists I was working with some years ago have now achieved a different degree of visibility within the art world, people like Martin Creed and Jeremy Deller, Chris Offili or Peter Doig. I never instructed people to make a publication, although a lot of people did. For me it was interesting to ask artists to step outside their studio or mainstream exhibiting practice, to think about a way to manifest their work for a different kind of culture that would be distributed in a different way and would be acknowledged and received in a different way.

Another aspect of Imprint 93, I guess is just me thinking about or being aware of earlier strategies from the 60s and 70s, about how and where the work might manifest itself; what work means when it manifests itself in a different context. For the last seven years the Guardian every Valentine's day publishes a section of Valentine's messages. I used to read these things for the kind of language that's used. Brevity's quite interesting because you're paying for it so it adds a different tone to it. A lot of them read to me as similar to the kind of language that was being used in art around that time, mid-90s. I started to commission artists to make text works for this space: I paid for them on my credit card. (reads through examples: Elizabeth Peyton / Gareth Jones / Jeremy Deller). I've worked with Jeremy Deller a lot. I do think Jeremy Deller's practice represents an interesting contemporaneous response to some of the things that conceptual work proposed. These are never announced, they were never announced, only in situations like this after the event. There's been four others, but I never tell anybody that I've done it or who I've done it with or where it was.

At this time I started making exhibitions. I think the term 'curator' is attached to me much later. This is the first of the exhibitions I made. (Slide) Again, I was thinking about earlier strategies of exhibition making and what constitutes an exhibition and it was also really about dealing with the limitations of the given situations. This was one of a series of exhibitions called 'Weekenders' that were held in my friend Peter Doig's Kings Cross studio. Originally I planned to make some work in the studio, but it was around the time I decided I didn't want to make art. So I asked four artists to make new work. One of the things that interests me most is curating new work with people. The 'Weekenders' came from my interest in Northern Soul music, Northern Soul Weekenders, where people from very diverse backgrounds would go to a place and congregate around things for a 48 hour period then disperse back to their regular lives. I wanted to see if it was possible to contain something of that atmosphere within an exhibition. So I commissioned four projects from artists to think about this situation. Again, I've always been very interested in printed ephemera, so I was kind of fetishising the printed material before the thing had even happened.

(Slide) This was Jeremy Deller's thing from '94 called 'Search for Bez'. Bez was the dancer in the Manchester band The Happy Mondays, Black Grape hadn't formed at this time. Jeremy went to Manchester with a video camera and monitor and just wondered around Manchester town centre and anyone he bumped into, he would just say to them, 'Have you seen Bez?' Most people didn't know what he was talking about but some people did and directed him to various points in the city and the map was drawn by Jeremy's cousins. It features places like the Hacienda, G-Mex, Dry Bar, places where Bez might be. He didn't find Bez but the video ends in a pub with Jeremy pointing his camera at the next table, and it's the Stone Roses. So that was as near as he got. The exhibition itself was like faux-museology. So we made this crude mannequin of a raver circa '88: we were trying to get the look of the local history museum where they try really hard to get it right and get it completely wrong. There was an education room, a reading room, which is essential these days in art galleries in case you don't understand the art. There was a table which features every copy of the NME which featured the Happy Mondays. That was the authoritative literature on the Happy Mondays. I asked all of the artists who made these Weekenders, to make a work that could be taken away by people who came to the show –

I'm very interested in gift exchange and it seems to me that's how things work out professionally, it's all to do with exchange. So people took these masks away (talks about 'Bez masks'...) (Slide) Years later at a Black Grape concert, here's Jeremy Deller presenting Bez with a Bez mask. So that was the end of the search for Bez.

Every year there used to be an Imprint 93 show where I just invited the artists I'd worked with to do whatever they wanted. Just trying to show some historical slippages. This is a piece (slide) by Stewart Home, it's called the 'Art Strike Bed': it was an attempt to revive Gustav Metzger's Art Strike from the late 1970s. Stewart decided to flier around the underground communities to suggest this three year termination of cultural production. The aim was worth thinking about. Of course, Stewart was the only person who did it. He claimed he spent most of the three years in (this) bed. The text says that he spent these three years reading Hegel and watching Kung-Fu movies. (On the left) a work by Jeremy Deller, which is a series of fictive posters for exhibitions he wants to see happen, but have yet to happen. He thinks or imagines that one day they might: an exhibition of the collected lyrics of Morrissey to be held at the British Museum. These are just displayed normally on noticeboards in art galleries. (Slides) This is for a Keith Moon retrospective at the Tate Gallery; this is an installation by Jeremy in Paris as part of an exhibition called 'Live/Life': a sort of survey of British art practice of the mid-90s which I was involved with in another capacity. Jeremy tried to turn the chic cafeteria downstairs in the Museum of Modern Art, Paris, into a kind of student refectory, with lots of these fake posters. The one I really love is 'The World of Gazza', for a show about Gazza to be held at the Museum of Mankind (laughter) which would be a really great exhibition. He re-showed this poster in Middlesbrough Art Gallery as part of a curated project by Sarah Staton. He put it up on the noticeboard of the Middlesbrough Art Gallery with all the other local information and posters and underneath he put a piece of paper saying 'we're taking a minibus down to this exhibition. If anyone is interested in coming, sign below'. It was really sad, about thirty people signed. It seemed like such a reasonable proposition.

This is an exhibition I made for Norwich Gallery, which maybe explains a lot of my thinking. It was called 'Imprint 93 and Other Related Ephemera'. The exhibition itself was a time line around the gallery from '91 to '97 (describes exhibition). Because Norwich Gallery's connected to an art school, I was trying to make an exhibition which had a kind of educational aspect to it, some kind of pedagogical twist. I was trying to reveal the straightforward mechanics of how people move through time, how artists find themselves in situations and why they find themselves in those situations. So beginning in '91 lots of groups of artists....and then by '97 they're showing at Tate Gallery, Lisson Gallery or whatever. So if you just followed it through, you could actually see how exactly this had happened, where people had found themselves. If you unpackaged the whole thing, it was just a clear realisation of the passage through time of a generation of people. Above the line were various projects that had manifested out of things I'd been involved with. So somewhere between Billy Childish and Stephen Willats, that's where my interest in art lies and I don't differentiate between my interest in both. So the line ended with current projects, with a bulletin board of things that were on in London at that time. The rest of the exhibition was presentations of other people's publishing activities. I'm a really big fan of any kind of publishing activity.

(Slide) This is an exhibition I did in '97 at a place in London called The Approach. The gallery's above a bar and has a very good reputation for showing young painters. The guy that runs the space asked me to make an exhibition and I think the budget for the show in its entirety was £300. We had about two weeks to do it. My original plan was to make a 100 person group show of artists I was interested in. The only conditioning thing was that there was some use or implication of language, hence the exhibition's title 'A – Z', which was the alphabet. And it was subtitled 'Things to Look At and/or things to be Read' which was the title of a very famous show at the Dwan Gallery in New York in '62/3, which featured Dadaist works, Futurist works, very early conceptual works. So it was just an exhibition for me to reveal my interests publicly, but at the same time, it was trying to look in a very straightforward fashion at how language has settled in current practice. The exhibition included a number of older practitioners such as Richard Hamilton, Stephen Willats, Ian Breakwell, Amikam Torem. A lot of younger artists, I guess mid-generation artists now: people like Liam Gillick, Tacita Dean, Martin Creed and also a lot of people I was teaching at the time. I have a very bad habit of showing people I teach. I really like shows that are hung 'salon' style, partly because it allows me to create historical slippages.

Recently I started making work again: I like my own work now, I never used to. It's sort of parodic, or it looks parodic of conceptual art. It certainly employs all of the visual charges of conceptual work. (Slide of show at Anthony Wilkinson Gallery in 1999.) The works are invariably just title pages from books: it's found text work, found conceptual art.

SUNE NORDGREN (CHAIRING THE DISCUSSION):

Actually when you listen to these two presentations there are lots of connections, a kind of conceptual attitude to art which is really interesting. There are more laughs for the recent work, and I suppose if Clive showed his pictures in the 70s there would have been lots of laughs as well. So this is really interesting, to see if the attitude has changed, the way everything, even small pieces of paper like Matthew puts together, they become museum pieces.

They lose some kind of 'energy' of course. (addresses Clive Phillpot) Do you think the attitude has changed?

CLIVE PHILLPOT:

I've been waiting for twenty years for this to happen. It seemed to me it was such a radical time: that's what interested me about 'Live in Your Head'. It was a time when things changed dramatically, first politically and socially, but also in the art world. And artists' attitudes to materials, the media and context all changed. That's why I was so happy to do this show. Then the ideas went underground in the 80s – this is a caricature of course – and neo-Expressionism came back with Reagan and Thatcher. And then suddenly it all caught up again. I was so excited to come back to this country and find young artists making similar kinds of work. To me it's just part of this ongoing heritage. This shift in art is really going to go forward for a long time.

MATTHEW HIGGS:

I think one of the things that's rarely acknowledged – and it hasn't really been acknowledged in a lot of the museum representations of conceptual work, certainly in the last decade, starting in 1990 with ARC in Paris' 'L'Art Conceptuél' and through MOCA Los Angeles' 'Reconsidering the Object of Art' and 'Global Conceptualism' at the Queens' Museum, and we can discuss it in relation to 'Live in Your Head' – is that the role of humour in early conceptual art has rarely been addressed and it certainly hasn't been written about in a particularly interesting way as a kind of tendency within the work itself. I think, as someone who was sixteen in 1980, when the 'classic' period of conceptual art had kind of been closed, my interest in thinking about these things, it was more about where ideas of desire and pleasure were also implicated alongside a kind of criticality. It's often the more 'marginal' artists – ie. artists who have become marginalised within the canon of conceptual work – that I find most interesting. People like Mark Camille Chaimowicz, where somehow there's something very different going on in the work and it was obviously very different at the time. There was a mischievous sense of something in the work that added to its criticality. So for me the Burgin tendency – if you could describe it as such – I find increasingly less interesting. Whilst it's of historical interest, it seems to me that the work that makes sense to artists now is the work that embraced pleasure and desire and humour.

SUNE NORDGREN:

But it wasn't less humorous?

CLIVE PHILLPOT:

This work or the former work?

SUNE NORDGREN:

The former work.

CLIVE PHILLPOT:

No, you had to look for it. If you go through Lucy Lippard's book 'Six Years', there's a lot of stuff there that may not necessarily mean to be funny, but it's like somehow real life is right at the fore and the core of – for convenience I'll call it conceptual art – but it's not just that. And that experiment in the mid-'60s was somehow getting closer to real life by different means, and that included passion and humour...by whatever means, any means.

SUNE NORDGREN:

What about the political aspects?

CLIVE PHILLPOT:

Well I wanted to make sure that they were included in the show and it was to some extent the more overtly political things about racism, dictatorships in Latin America. Although the exhibition was supposed to be based in Britain, I was determined to include work that was not British in it. So all the foreign artists in 'Portrait of Robin Crozier' and someone like the Argentinean David Lamelas, who were not British but were part of art in Britain, were all included. It seemed to me there was a watershed around 1970, when art became more overtly politicised. So Conrad Atkinson was in there, plus the 'Women in Work' piece which was very much more political and in fact tested the parameters of art, in the sense of whether it was politics or art. Then I think the biggest thing of all was Feminism, which came in like a rush as far as I could see after 1970. It was wonderful to me, to get involved with that again after feeling it in New York in the 70s and 80s, when it was still very strong, (political protest was also very strong then in New York), and to try to put it in a show. Although in the end what you're left with is just these artefacts around the walls.

SUNE NORDGREN (TO MATTHEW HIGGS):

It's a completely different attitude now isn't it; it's more difficult to be political today isn't it, when left is not left and right is not right anymore?

MATTHEW HIGGS:

I guess the most apparent manifestation of the problems that face artists when they confront politics is in Vienna, having just been there two weeks ago, sat in the audience of a place called 'The Depot' where they've been having these political discussions on a weekly basis. It seemed to me at some point that the discussion was kind of exhausting itself because there was no way to effect change apart from to keep acknowledging resistance. I think Jeremy Deller's quite an interesting artist in this respect. In his project for the Tate in July with Alan Kane where they're setting up an archive of Contemporary Folk Art – ie. only folk art made in 1999 – 2000 – they have an exquisite banner from the Brixton bombing. It's a reflection of a grass roots folk art: how folk art responds to contemporary political scenarios. The curatorial students' exhibition last year at the Royal College of Art was called 'Democracy' and was about socially engaged art. It was trying to examine current art and was informed by conceptual strategies relating to a political identity. It seems to me that how artists politicise their work now is problematic, because we don't exist in a politicised culture as we might have done in the 60s or 70s. But of course I don't know that because I wasn't around at the time. But certainly as a teenager I used to find myself on CND marches and when I was (at) Newcastle in '84 when the miners' strikes were on, I remember that the Polytechnic Fine Art Department would, on a weekly basis, take two minibuses out on the picket lines. I've no idea whether they were glad to see us or not, but numbers make a difference. We did that every week and I can't imagine a minibus rolling up at Goldsmith's saying, 'we're gonna go and protest at the closure of an electronics manufacturing plant in Surrey': there'd be no one on the bus. So it seems to me that the decision to get on the bus has changed because the broader culture we exist in has changed. Then you had groups like 'Group Material' or 'General Idea', and I think that manifestation of the political/social responsibility for art is still pretty interesting.

SUNE NORDGREN:

I would very much like to involve you (to audience) of course as well. But I have one more question. Since this is also about curating, both Clive and Matthew come from different backgrounds as curators and I'm very curious about whether they feel it is an advantage, being an artist or being a librarian, a book person, coming from a different direction? Most of the curators doing shows in institutions have another, more academic background. Is it an advantage or a disadvantage being outside?

CLIVE PHILLPOT:

I'd say it would have been an advantage if I'd let myself go. I felt like I should respect some sort of curatorial expertise, but I realise now that if I'd had my head that show ('Live in Your Head') would have been completely different. I'd done one show on that scale before, on Fluxus, at the Museum of Modern Art in New York, actually in the library, which was natural to Fluxus as there were so many documents. But we also had performance and film shows to go with it. It too was a collaboration, and I should say that collaborations can have a potential to make something happen that wouldn't happen otherwise. But I think I've kind of respected the game that other people played, but I shouldn't have. But I would expect if I really felt that I had a free hand and wasn't given a structure at the beginning, I would do something very different. I hope I get that opportunity some time.

SUNE NORDGREN:

Working more closely with the artists you mean?

CLIVE PHILLPOT:

It could be with the artists; it could be using a space with some sort of function within the tradition of the gallery that is not like what you've seen before. I felt that if I could have pushed the structure, pushed the team there, I could have done something very different. But I respected the fact that I was working within the stream of exhibitions in an institution: people have roles to play. But it might be nice to shake all that up; maybe one who was trained as a curator doesn't get that feeling?

SUNE NORDGREN:

I think this is something the ICA is starting to do by having four curators...

MATTHEW HIGGS:

Well I've only worked institutionally for the last year. Particularly with starting to work on the British Art Show under the auspices of the Arts Council, and then very recently I've found myself as one of 4 curators – Directors of Exhibitions is the title we've been given – at the ICA. Our programme starts in November, so we're currently in the midst of some quite complex emotional logistics about how four people from very different backgrounds should work together, with somebody based in Amsterdam, somebody based in Glasgow, somebody based in Paris, and myself coming from London. And my understanding of why the ICA might have proposed that model within London's culture – and maybe we could expand it out but I might as well talk about it in terms of London's exhibition culture – is that with the opening of Tate Modern, every institution of a certain size in London, such as the Whitechapel, Camden Arts Centre, South London Gallery, the Serpentine, are all radically having to rethink what they're doing. There are two straightforward reasons for this: one is that the kind of exhibitions that probably haven't happened in London may start to become manifest. But there's also an economic impetus: that Tate Modern's ability to absorb sponsorship is seen as a real threat to these other places. So the ICA's introduced this model, which is largely untested as far as I'm aware, as a way of making a break with an earlier kind of curatorial model – working with a single curator who largely dictated the programme – to working with something that's much more fragmented, that's informed by other disciplines and contexts, by bringing together different respective attitudes towards exhibition-making. Whether we're the right four people to be doing it is another question and whether the infrastructure at the ICA can deal with it, again is another question. But for me it's a big shock because for the last ten years I just sort of pottered about on my own and pretty much paid for everything myself. I've realised about one hundred projects with artists. I like working with artists and I like making new work, wherever that work takes place, whether it's in a newspaper or an exhibition or whatever.

This is my first job, at the ICA. I've really never had a job before. It's just a shock: bureaucracy, fundraising and administration terrify me because I've never done them before. I know why I haven't done them before: it's because they terrify me, but now I find myself having to do it. And all of a sudden, in a really simple way, it tempers your relationship with art, or it changes your fundamental relationship with doing something. Certainly the way that I've worked is that I've talked about doing something with an artist and we'd do it. That was it, it happened. And you can't proceed that way within an institution because there's all these other things that impact upon it. So for me it's a learning process and maybe in five years time I'll think it was a fundamentally good thing but at the moment it doesn't feel like that. Because it's not my relationship to or understanding of art at all. But I can see it's certainly how art gets presented to the public on a larger scale.

SUNE NORDGREN:

I think that the ICA's 'experiment', whatever you might call it, is interesting and perhaps other institutions can benefit from it as well. (To audience) Any questions?

QUESTION:

I'd like to ask about Jeremy Deller and Martin Creed.
Where was the link in communication that got those two
situations to the Tate from what seems like a microcosm
that they've generally been working in? What I mean is, the
Tate is like this big, abstract thing and of course it must be
made up of hundreds of people who somehow now must
be infiltrating beyond what we're used to them doing...?

MATTHEW HIGGS:

Well, they're clearly re-branding. I don't know if you've
ever encountered the workings of the Tate Gallery. I was
involved with a publication last year and it's mind-
blowingly complicated to get anything done. It's extraordinary: you can't believe how long it takes to get something
really simple done. I guess in a sense it was them letting
their hair down to some degree by letting Martin and
Jeremy into the building. But at the same time I think it's
much broader than that. I think it does represent a shift or
a perception of recent, young British art. It's an early step
but I think it's a drift away from previous perception of the
yBa, Sarah Lucas or Matt Collishaw, that generation.
I think there's an incremental idea that while Jeremy
(Deller) and Martin Creed's work is quite well acknowledged in mainland Europe and in New York and LA, it's
like a belated acknowledgement of the fact that they've
worked independently for ten years on a very low
economy. So they're useful to the Tate as I think the Tate
is useful to them.

SUNE NORDGREN:

But there is a desperation in England as well, to find
something. Is there life after the yBa's?

MATTHEW HIGGS:

Yes, there's this show at the Tate (Britain) which opens in a few weeks, a triennial I think, called 'New British Art 2000'. It's curated by Charles Esche and Virginia Button, and it presents artists of different generations. One aspect of that project is to try to collapse that homogenous idea of the mid-90s generation orbiting around Damien Hirst. I guess it's Tate Britain's problem ultimately, how to deal with British art of the last twenty years, whether that's art made by Susan Hiller or art made by Jeremy Deller. It seems very schizophrenic to me, but it's early days.

QUESTION:

I also saw your [Clive's] exhibition. I was really interested in the publications. I thought it was a real pity you presented them in the way you did, which happens very often in exhibitions. I wanted to ask you, is this because librarians want to keep the books for themselves? Because you were saying you also used photocopies for artworks, so why didn't you make exhibition copies of the books themselves? You can see reproductions of artworks, but those things (artists' books) you can hardly ever find...

QUESTION:

Can I just add a footnote to this? Clive, remind me about this. Weren't you involved in one of the earliest shows of artists' books? And didn't that show provide copies for people to look at, and read and tear out pages if they wanted to? So, what intervened in your thinking or was this an institutional problem?

CLIVE PHILLPOT:

It was partly that. But to me, I was also playing against type. Everyone expects me to do book shows and I

thought, 'the last thing I want to do is a book show'.
That's partly why I thought the magazines in a sense were
something I'd rather lay emphasis on. It was very unfortu-
nate there was just this tail of books out in the lobby. Of
course, if there had been more focus on that then I think
you would have had to had things to handle, I'm all for that.

QUESTION:

But it also provides background information...

CLIVE PHILLPOT:

I was against that, quite honestly. I wanted a more visual
experience, so I was quite happy not to have books in that
respect. It seemed to me those works on the wall and on
the floor are something you can deal with, as 'real art'.
But I didn't want to bring reference books, or bring a
reading room and all that kind of stuff... There were not
many informative labels and that was partly time; we ran
out of time to write all the labels. It didn't bother me too
much: if people have enough curiosity, there are ways they
can find things. I was all for the paramountcy of the works.
So I personally didn't want to clutter them up with ancillary
things to read as well. The artists' books were a gesture,
to say 'these were important' and again it would have
been nice if you could have read some of them. But it was
such an arbitrary selection I didn't want to do anything
more than that.

QUESTION:

I know a lot about conceptual art, but some of the names
in that exhibition I hadn't heard about...

CLIVE PHILLPOT:

That was the point of the show.

QUESTION:

But I was interested to get more information, because they were artists who were not so well known. (CP holds up exhibition catalogue. Audience laughter)

QUESTION:

I'd like to ask Clive, having experienced being on both sides of the Atlantic, obviously there has been this movement within Britain in recent years, but whether there had been a similar scene of artists' publications in New York?

CLIVE PHILLPOT:

That's been pretty consistent I think. In fact, there's this book store in Manhattan called 'Printed Matter' founded by Sol LeWitt and Lucy Lippard, which is an institution that has no equal here or almost anywhere. I find it very difficult to find stuff anymore. I feel like I can't write about artists' books because I can't find them anymore. There I was living on top of it. The phenomenon went in cycles, my enthusiasm went in cycles too, and it's still busy and active. I, like Matthew, am fascinated by printed art, as well as art on the wall. It's very difficult to find it in this country now. Libraries are building it up, but you've got to seek the libraries out. It's not like a bookstore you can just walk into.

MATTHEW HIGGS:

I guess the most obvious manifestation – although I don't have a computer so I don't know about these things – is the internet. It's obviously where something happens but I've never been there so I don't know.

CLIVE PHILLPOT:

I don't feel that's quite the same. People talk about books on the internet, I don't feel that's quite the same experience, without wishing to be antideluvian or something. What you have in your hand is very different from what you can scroll. Scrolling seems to me such a backward step. I wish there were a more interactive way of dealing with that.

QUESTION:

I just wanted to ask Matthew...in relation to someone like Martin Creed, who portrays quite a lot of independence but is on fact represented by a 'blue chip' gallery in London....

MATTHEW HIGGS:

I'll reveal my interest: I'm one of the three people that run the 'blue chip gallery' (The Cabinet Gallery) – it's far from 'blue' in my thinking about it. It's only in the last twelve months that he (Martin Creed) has made anything you would describe as money, i.e. he can now afford to live in a manner that's reasonable and decent – and he's not unique. It's by no means high-faluting. Something that's not acknowledged anywhere, is the relatively desperate economy that still exists in the art world, for most artists. Within this fantasy of the yBa, many of the successful artists you associate with the yBa's are effectively still living on an economy equivalent to their student days. This is ten-twelve years on; these people are in their mid-thirties. Now, how do we resolve that, maybe we don't? I think especially, living in London, it's so extraordinarily expensive. I find it frightening how expensive it is to live in London now. It's difficult for me to see how London can sustain a community of younger artists anymore, if the current economic climate continues to exist. Within British art, if it returns to its early '70s 'wilderness', it will be simply because the economic climate in London is preventing young artists from being able to sustain a life and a studio practice of any kind. It really is a fact. In '91 Martin Creed graduated from the Slade BA and he started showing seriously straight away. But it took eight years before he had a commercial gallery exhibition that made money. That's a decent amount of time.

CLIVE PHILLPOT:

What came to mind when you were saying that, was Lawrence Weiner, who in '68 published the radical book 'Statements'. But he was still living like a student twenty years later. He didn't make any money for ages. Partly because he was making site-specific work and things that could be not be bought.

MATTHEW HIGGS:

Isn't his famous comment something like, 'if you can under-stand the work, you own it'? That kind of excludes sales!

QUESTION:

Do you see it as a commercial gallery 'letting its hair down' a little bit, offering something that's 'uncommer-cial'? It's kind of weird that Clive should say that some of these artists you look at all around the world...they sort of disappear [if] they're not in London...People do disappear sometimes...

MATTHEW HIGGS:

There are artists who self-consciously disappear. There's artists like Stanley Brouwn in Amsterdam or David Hammons in New York. These are artists who self-consciously resist the system as it's presented to them. Obviously that's one way of dealing with the art world's economy or strategies. But I think another thing that's never universally acknowledged is that a lot of the key developments in contemporary art take place in commercial galleries. Certainly if you look at the European dissemination of conceptual art, it was almost entirely within commercial galleries such as Konrad Fischer or Wide White Space. A gallery like Cabinet, which is the gallery I work with, from its outset in the early 90s, was always seen as an institution that had a very different idea of what it was thinking about as a gallery. And I think (it's the same for) Nicholas Logsdail's Lisson Gallery in the early 70s/late 60s, that the liberty presented by a commercial situation where you're not inhibited by public funding or answerable to public funding or any kind of ideology, allows that to be an incredibly experimental space, providing that the owner can sustain his economy. So often a lot of the key developments in contemporary art did take place within commercial situations. It didn't mean that they generated cash, but that's the arena they often took place in.

CLIVE PHILLPOT:

I would contrast that with the turn of the 60s/70s decade where there was a radical scene at Gallery House which was not commercial, it was like a squat and yet this was a most important space. And the other show that always meant a lot to me was 'Art Spectrum' at Alexandra Palace: there was Art Spectrum London, Art Spectrum South East, North, Wales, Scotland and so on. Something like an Expo was taken over by artists to do whatever they liked in their booths. It was one of the most eye-opening shows I've ever seen, with probably 200-300 artists there. And there was 'Fluxshoe', which was disseminating Fluxus ideas in Britain, which was just a band of people wondering around the country. So at that time, by contrast – I'm sure it's not as simple as that – there were a lot of things that were not to do with commercial galleries. I think the kind of freedom you might get from a commercial gallery, may or may not be a different kind of freedom from the kind you get when you've got enough space, run by artists. I think it may be exaggerating to say you get a particular freedom in a commercial set up.

QUESTION:

Surely the 'conservative factor' if you like, comes more from institutions in the sense of museums. If you look back to before WW1 even, exhibitions curated by artists, big artist-run manifestations and small supposedly commercial endeavours, which in fact didn't make any money, were where the exciting things were happening. But the museums were very slow to catch up, if catch up is even the right word. To go back to Matthew's point, about these younger artists appearing at the Tate, does that tell us anything really about the institution, or is it more about a problem for the artists to be seen in that context? Is it at all problematic to go on producing work that has some kind of radical, playful edge once you're within the institution to that extent?

MATTHEW HIGGS:

Well, to talk about a specific example, with Jeremy Deller and Alan Kane's project (as part of 'New British Art 2000' at Tate Britain), the Tate are charging £6 to get into this exhibition. It's their fee-charging exhibition so the general visitor would have to make that decision. I think £6 is a lot of money for this kind of show when 'Between a Cinema and a Hard Place' at Tate Modern is only £3.

One of the communities Jeremy and Alan are working with is a community in the Lake District. I don't know the details, but it would appear the whole village is just making Folk Art the whole time. And Jeremy and Alan said very straightforwardly, 'these are the artists, there are, say one hundred of them and they're to be shown as artists, and they all get free passes to the exhibition, because they are artists who are showing their work at the Tate Gallery'. But the Tate aren't letting them in for free. So immediately there's this idea of authorship in relation to the work. And Jeremy and Alan are pretty clear about whose work this is. Another thing they wanted to do was to invite the local WI flower-arranging group from Pimlico: every week in the foyer of the Tate Gallery there would be a different floral display done in relation to a current news item, which is what these WI people do. The Tate said, 'this is impossible, it's too complicated'. Jeremy said, 'they're just gonna arrange some flowers and put them on a plinth in the foyer', and the people at Tate said, 'how will the audience know it's art?' (Audience laughter) They didn't know where to put the label or what to put on the label. And Jeremy and Alan said, 'it isn't art, it's a floral display by the local Women's Institute made in response to a current news item, full stop'. And it seems to me that at that point, do Jeremy and Alan leave the institution and say we're compromising our desires and intentions, or do we say that ultimately this is a much larger platform and audience for this kind of activity and may contribute to change? So there's that moment when I guess you have to accept compromise.

SUNE NORDGREN:

But should you?

MATTHEW HIGGS:

Should you, of course, yes.

QUESTION:

That's a really nice positive answer. But perhaps because I'm somewhat older I see a slightly sinister edge to the role of these large institutions embracing what they see as the very, very latest thing. I think it takes away from the impact of the ideas. I think that ideas represent a community, they go out to larger communities and when they finally end up so diffuse then they really become something different. It's just a very interesting thing, we're at a very interesting time with all this. The Tate is a very old institution. The fact that it's rushing to embrace young artists must surely mean something.

CLIVE PHILLPOT:

But it may depend on the integrity of the artists in the sense that they can deal with this apparent success and then go away and do the same thing they did before. It's like Hans Haacke being used by a museum and then walking away and doing what he wants to do. So it needn't be the end of a wonderful career.

QUESTION:

Well it might be interesting to point out that Hans Haacke is not in the Museum of Modern Art's collection. He's allowed in and out of exhibitions but art history is built up on more permanent instances. These things are very interesting that you brought up, coming out of Clive's initial comment that many of the artists in the show he put together at the Whitechapel, seem to have somehow disappeared. It certainly doesn't mean they've disappeared as artists. They may be doing fantastic work outside a capital city somewhere.

CLIVE PHILLPOT:

That also reinforces what I said. The fickleness of the art world or the media very often allows that to happen. But that's also ok for the artists if they want to pursue their work and not deviate because of these flashy moments they might have on the façade of the Tate or something.

QUESTION:

Isn't that related to the freedom of the market?

MATTHEW HIGGS:

I think that certain work has its moment and it's so exquisitely connected to that moment that that's the time it should take place. We have this strange idea that art should be forever, that its inherent quality means that it's forever. I certainly don't want the Bachmann Tuner Overdrive rock group to be hanging around now. They were perfect at the time, they did what they had to do and then they dispersed. I know the record lives on just as artists' work in a catalogue lives on but I think this idea that art is for all times is actually not so true. It diminishes the interest in some of the art I find most interesting. Öyvind Fahlström's a really good example from my understanding of the work: that this work had extraordinary moments and it was so explicitly connected to those moments. Looking at the work now, having the opportunity to look at the work now – which is great for someone like me who wasn't around to see the work – seeing the installation show in Cologne, it's fantastic to have the opportunity to reconsider things in a contemporary moment. But that doesn't mean everything should be around for all time. I'm really excited when things disappear. I'm really glad when things bob under the surface, because they no longer have anything to say. And then when they reappear, it's often all the more exciting. Some things, you know, I'm glad are gone. (Audience laughter)

QUESTION:

Can I just say something here about the idea of audience. Seeing the 'Sensation' show at the Royal Academy, to me it was all 'dead' because I'd seen all that work before as an artist going to exhibitions and seeing Rachel

Whiteread's 'House' in Chisenhale' and the other work in exhibitions in more 'alternative' spaces. But put all together in the Royal Academy it was dead. And then with the public coming in who regard an exhibition as an encapsulated moment, would experience it in their own way. It's to do with at what point you're entering that dialogue, if you like. It's also to do with how the audience sees it and more people are going to go to Tate Modern than are going to search out a small gallery that's showing one piece by somebody.

MATTHEW HIGGS:

But I think in institutions in this country – specifically Tate, but it's much wider – there's such a nervousness on the part of institutions to do interesting shows. In a ten-year period the Tate Gallery made three exhibitions of international contemporary art, in a ten-year period. Now that is disgusting, there's no other way round it. That is just appalling. Stuart Morgan's 'Rites of Passage' was a fantastic exhibition, 'Abracadabra' was a less than fantastic exhibition but at least it had it's moments and, I can't even remember if there was a third one, maybe it's two...

QUESTION:

'Paris Post-War', that was another one.

MATTHEW HIGGS:

Ok, post-war, that's stretching it. It does strike me as extraordinary that given the prominence or visibility of the generation of artists who emerged in the years after '88 – I said this in the British Art show catalogue – there hasn't been an institutional exhibition of Sarah Lucas' work, Gillian Wearing's work, Douglas Gordon's work etc. They've had ten years to do these shows, they would have been massively popular exhibitions and nobody's done it.

So these exhibitions take place in the Boymans Museum....

QUESTION:

Well, there have been quite a few in Liverpool. You may need to leave the centre sometimes to see some good international art, because London is so London-centred.

MATTHEW HIGGS:

I think the saddest thing about Tate Liverpool – I visit pretty much everything they do – is their current ad in 'Frieze', which says 'just three hours from London'. I think that was the weakest thing I've ever seen an institution do to be honest.

QUESTION:

I'm not talking about since the London Tate has opened. I'm talking about the last ten years.

MATTHEW HIGGS:

Sure, I mean Tate Liverpool's committed to only hosting exhibitions that are generated in Liverpool. They're not interested in taking stuff from Tate London. But I think they've really let themselves down with that advert. To put on your advert, above the artists' names, 'only three hours from London' is pretty weak.

QUESTION:

However, they managed to show Polke in this country, they managed to show Douglas Gordon and Gary Hill, Bill Viola, so I think there have been some interesting shows conducted. The Serpentine is also showing Jane & Louise Wilson, Gillian Wearing.... so I don't agree with you these artists haven't been shown enough.

CLIVE PHILLPOT:

Can I comment on something Matthew said about art not being forever – he didn't quite say it like that – and also artists not necessarily being relevant for more than a moment when they connect with this audience? To me, the most fascinating artists are those who have ups and downs and ins and outs, who are engaged and not engaged in the art world. Two artists who fascinate me are Gustav Metzger, who's been off the map and almost never on the map in some sense, and my current preoccupation, Ray Johnson, who avoided museums, avoided galleries. (You can even go back to someone like Hogarth who had a life that was sometimes engaged and sometimes not engaged with the public sphere.) And yet – and that's why I mentioned the word integrity earlier – looking at their work and the distance they've travelled, you can see that they have an integrity and their work is growing and developing all the time. Whether or not it engages with the moment, the particular media moment, whatever that might be. I think that needs to be set alongside what Matthew was saying.

SUNE NORDGREN:

So why can't all the poor artists in London move to the North East? It's much cheaper here. (Audience laughter)

Thanks to speakers and audience applause.

BIOGRAPHIES

MATTHEW HIGGS:

Matthew Higgs studied painting at Newcastle Polytechnic in the late 1980s. He now works as an artist, a curator, a writer and a publisher of artists' books. In 2000 he was appointed Associate Director of Exhibitions at the ICA in London, as well as working as one of the selectors of the fifth British Art Show and co-curating (with Paul Noble) the exhibition 'Protest and Survive' at the Whitechapel Art Gallery, London (September – November 2000).

SUSAN HILLER:

Artist Susan Hiller holds the newly created Chair, BALTIC Professor of Contemporary Art, at the University of Newcastle's Department of Fine Art. Susan Hiller's audio-sculpture 'Witness', commissioned by Artangel, was included in 'Intelligence: New British Art 2000' at Tate Britain and will travel to the Habana Biennial. Her video installation 'Wild Talents' was selected for the Fifth British Art Show. The large-scale touring exhibition 'Dream Machines', which she curated, is currently at Camden Arts Centre in London.

JAMES LINGWOOD:

James Lingwood has been a Co-Director of London-based commissioning agency Artangel since 1991. Artangel commissions outside conventional gallery spaces have included Rachel Whiteread's 'House' (1993/4), Matthew Barney's film 'Cremaster 4' (1995), Ilya and Emilia Kabakov's 'Palace of Projects' (1998) and Douglas Gordon's 'Feature Film' (1999). James Lingwood has also organised many major exhibitions of contemporary art including retrospective surveys of the work of Thomas Schütte, Juan Munõz and Thomas Struth.

PROFESSOR JOHN MILNER:

John Milner is Professor of Art History at the University of Newcastle-upon-Tyne. His numerous publications include studies of the art of the early Soviet period ('Kazmir Malevich and the Art of Geometry', 1996, and 'A Dictionary of Russian and Soviet Artists', 1993) and on late nineteenth-century Paris in 'The Studios of Paris: The Capital of Art in the Late Nineteenth Century' (1988).

SUNE NORDGREN:

Sune Nordgren was appointed the first Director of BALTIC Centre for Contemporary Art, Gateshead, in 1997. Previously he was Director of Iaspis (International Artists Studio Programme in Sweden) and before that, of Malmö Konsthall, Malmö, Sweden, where he curated numerous exhibitions of contemporary artists including Richard Serra, Leon Golub, Cindy Sherman and Andres Serrano.

CLIVE PHILLPOT:

Clive Phillpot is the Librarian of the Visual Arts Department at the British Council in London and was previously Director of the Library at the Museum of Modern Art in New York. He has curated numerous exhibitions, including 'Networking' (1996) and more recently with Andrea Tarsia, the large-scale show of British conceptual art of the 1960s and 70s 'Live in Your Head' at the Whitechapel Art Gallery, London (Feb – April 2000).